BURTON W. FOLSOM, JR.

THE MYTH OF THE ROBBER BARONS

A New Look at the Rise of Big Business in America

SIXTH EDITION • FOREWORD BY FORREST MCDONALD

Manufactured in the United States of America

Published by *Young America's Foundation*
F. M. Kirby Freedom Center
110 Elden Street
Herndon, Virginia 20170

Library of Congress Cataloging-in-Publication Data

Folsom, Burton W.
(Entrepreneurs vs. the State)
The Myth of the Robber Barons/Burton W. Folsom, Jr.
p. cm.
Previously published as: Entrepreneurs vs. the State
ISBN 0-9630203-0-7 (HB) : $19.95. —ISBN 0-9630203-1-5 *(PB)* : $9.95
1. Capitalists and financiers—United States—History. 2. Competition—United States—History. 3. Free enterprise—History. 4. Steamboats—United States—History. 5. Entrepreneurship—History. I. Title
HG181.F647 1991
338'.04'097309034—dc20

Young America's Foundation
F.M. Kirby Freedom Center
110 Elden Street
Herndon, Virginia 20170
800-USA-1776
703-318-9122 (fax)
www.yaf.org

Reagan Ranch Center
217 State Street
Santa Barbara California 93101
888-USA-1776
www.reaganranch.org

To Anita

From reviews of THE MYTH OF THE ROBBER BARONS

"THE MYTH OF THE ROBBER BARONS is . . . excellent. . . . In short, this book is the perfect supplement to most standard economic and business history textbooks. This reviewer has adopted it already."

Larry Schweikart, THE HISTORIAN

"I read this book in one sitting. In spite of the easy reading of the text, the book has profound meaning for the nature of business in America, with implications for political philosophy and economic theory. There isn't a businessman in the country who would not profit from the reading of this important book."

Angus MacDonald, BOOK REVIEWS

"Folsom demonstrates the pernicious effects of government involvement in business. . . . The enormous value of this book is that it enlightens the intelligent reader with the facts about an era that virtually every history book shrouds in falsehoods."

Second Renaissance Books

THE MYTH OF THE ROBBER BARONS "is a lively, well written and informative introduction to the subject. It is a useful source for students of American history."

Ann M. Scanlon, NEW YORK HISTORY

"The subtlest essay makes James J. Hill an American hero as the only man who built a transcontinental railroad without government subsidy. . . . The most daring attempt at revision is the author's paean to John D. Rockefeller."

Stuart D. Brandes, AMERICAN HISTORICAL REVIEW

"Folsom draws an insightful lesson. Government aid [to railroads] bred inefficiency; the inefficiency raised costs and rates, and angry customers demanded government regulation; the resulting regulation promoted even greater inefficiency. . . ."

Robert Higgs, THE WORLD & I

"Burt Folsom has done a wonderful job. . . . The picture of economic history printed in this book helps prove that political promotion of economic development is futile."

Carl Watner, THE VOLUNTARYIST

"Folsom presents the subjects as they were, warts and all, avoiding shrill accusation or exoneration of shortcomings."

Tommy W. Rogers, CHRONICLES

"If these stories are correct, then much of the conventional history of American business is off base. . . . Folsom persuasively describes how government subsidies to 'political entrepreneurs' actually lowered the quality of output."

M. L. Rantala, CHICAGO ENTERPRISE

Contents

CHAPTER SIX

CHAPTER SEVEN

APPENDIX

Foreword

It is possible to regard this book as light reading, despite the range and depth of the meticulous scholarship on which it is based, because it is written in a pleasant, almost chatty style and is concerned with an array of fascinating characters—bold innovators who created mightily as well as pious frauds who bilked the public on a grand scale. Indeed, though I have studied American economic history for many years, I have found on almost every page information and anecdotes I had not encountered before. The entertainment value of the work is not lessened by the fact that it revises in important ways many misperceptions that historians have imposed upon the record—for instance, the idea that vertical mobility is a myth. Quietly but conclusively, and without interrupting the flow of his narrative, Folsom demonstrates that vertical mobility, both upwards and downwards, has truly been a norm in America: poor men have become rich men and rich men have become poor men, depending upon skill, brains, work, and luck.

But there is considerably more here than some good stories and some significant revisionism. On one level, Folsom shows that the "Robber Baron" school of historians of American business enterprise was partly right and partly wrong but was unable to distinguish which was which. He points out that during the nineteenth and the early twentieth century (and by unmistakable implication, in the late twentieth as well) there were two kinds of business developers, whom he describes as "political entrepreneurs" and "market entrepreneurs." The former were in fact comparable to medieval robber barons, for they sought and obtained wealth through the coercive power of the state, which is to say that they were subsidized by government and were sometimes granted monopoly status by government. Invariably, their products or services were inferior to and more expensive than the goods and services provided by market entrepreneurs, who sought and obtained wealth by producing more and better for less cost to the consumer. The market entrepreneurs, however, have been repeatedly—one is tempted to say systematically—ignored by historians.

On another level, Folsom's study has profound implications for American historiography beyond the immediate subject to which it is addressed. It is commonly held that the Whig Party of Clay and Webster and its successor Republican Party of Abraham Lincoln and William McKinley were the "pro-business" parties, and that the Jacksonian Democrats were anti-business. What comes through here is something quite different. The Whigs and Republicans engaged in a great deal of pro-business rhetoric and in talk of economic development, but the policies they advocated, such as subsidies, grants of special privileges, protective tariffs, and the like, actually worked to retard development and to stifle innovation. The Jacksonian Democrats engaged in a great deal of anti-business rhetoric, but the results of their policies were to remove or reduce governmental interferences into private economic activity, and thus to free market entrepreneurs to go about their creative work. The entire nation grew wealthy as a consequence.

On yet another level, though Folsom's work is balanced, judicious history, addressed to the past (and is unmarred by the shrill accusatory tone that characterizes the writings of anti-business historians), it has a powerful relevance to current political discourse. In response to the relative decline of the American economy during the last decade or two, many corporate businessmen have joined with leftist ideologues to clamor for a "partnership" between government and business that would involve central planning, protective tariffs, and a host of restrictions upon foreign competitors. What Folsom has to say to them is a common-sense message drawn from endlessly repeated historical examples. Political promotion of economic development is inherently futile, for it invariably rewards incompetence; if incompetence is rewarded, incompetence will be the product; and when incompetence is the product, politicians will insist that increased planning and increased regulation is the appropriate remedy.

Adam Smith forewarned us more than two centuries ago: "The statesman, who should attempt to direct people in what manner they ought to employ their capital, would not only load himself with a most unnecessary attention, but assume an authority which could safely be trusted, not only to no single person, but to no council or senate whatever, and which would nowhere be so dangerous as in the hands of a man who had folly and presumption enough to fancy himself fit to exercise it."

Forrest McDonald

Williamsburg, Virginia
April 1987

Preface to the Sixth Edition

I am delighted to welcome *The Myth of the Robber Barons* to a sixth edition. That it continues to sell well is testimony to the persistence of free market ideas. Special thanks go to the usual culprits: Ron Robinson for his patience and support for almost thirty years; Patrick Coyle for his energy and encouragement; and Dede Hamilton for all the time she takes with this book. Thanks also go to Larry Arnn, Larry Reed, Larry Schweikart, and Joseph Rishel for their advice and counsel. Over the years, I have benefited from suggestions and criticisms from Lee Benson, Roger Custer, Edward Davies II, Thomas DiLorenzo, James R. Edwards, Winston Elliott, Burton Folsom, Sr., Margaret Folsom, Samuel P. Hays, Robert Hessen, Rusty Humphries, Doug Jeffrey, Aileen Kraditor, Forrest and Ellen McDonald, William H. Mulligan, George Nash, James Nesbitt, Glenn Porter, Helen Roulston, Julius Rubin, James Taylor, John Willson, Kirby Wilbur, and my students at Murray State University and Hillsdale College.

In doing research, I needed help from many libraries and institutions. The Hagley Museum and Library in Wilmington, Delaware, gave me access to the Scranton papers and other specialized sources. The R. G. Dun Credit Reports in the Baker Library at Harvard University helped me in writing the Schwab and Scranton essays. The Library of Congress and the National Archives provided me with a wealth of sources on entrepreneurs. At the Lackawanna Historical Society, I received wise counsel from former directors Robert Mattes and William Lewis. William W. Scranton was very supportive and has straightened me out on some points about his family history. The libraries at Murray State University, Southern Illinois University, Indiana University, and Hillsdale College have supplied me with most of the secondary sources used in this study.

In the financing and publication of this book, I have received aid and comfort from Young America's Foundation, the Wilbur Foundation, Roe Foundation, Broyhill Foundation, the Bradley Foundation, and from both Murray State University and Hillsdale College.

Finally, I want to thank my wife Anita, for her wise counsel and editing skills, and my son Adam, who has my blog BurtFolsom.com up and running. Anita and Adam make this work worthwhile for me.

Burton W. Folsom, Jr.

Hillsdale, Michigan
March 2010

"The greatest anti-monopolist in the country"

The Bettmann Archive

Cornelius Vanderbilt (1794–1877), known as "Commodore Vanderbilt." The classic market entrepreneur.

CHAPTER ONE

Commodore Vanderbilt and the Steamship Industry

For two generations historians have been arguing about the effects of entrepreneurs on American industry. Whether the entrepreneurs were Robber Barons, industrial statesmen, or irrelevant to growth still seems to be disputed even after shelves of books have been written on the subject.[1] Maybe we can find a useful line of reasoning by looking at one of America's first large-scale businesses, the steamship industry. It was mechanized in the early 1800s; and, during that century, it was in the vanguard of technological change. Steamboating was also highly competitive and soon became large in scale. Furthermore, a look at the steamboat industry allows us to study entrepreneurs in the comparative context of the whole industry. Only then can we see how different entrepreneurs responded to different challenges and who, if any, made creative contributions to industrial growth.[2]

A key point about the steamship industry is that the government played an active role right from the start in both America and England. Right away this separates two groups of entrepreneurs—those who sought subsidies and those who didn't. Those who tried to succeed in steamboating primarily through federal aid, pools, vote buying, or stock speculation we will classify as *political entrepreneurs*. Those who tried to succeed in steamboating primarily by creating and marketing a superior product at a low cost we will classify as *market entrepreneurs*. No entrepreneur fits perfectly into one category or the other, but most fall generally into one category or the other. The political entrepreneurs often fit the classic Robber Baron mold;

they stifled productivity (through monopolies and pools), corrupted business and politics, and dulled America's competitive edge. Market entrepreneurs, by contrast, often made decisive and unpredictable contributions to American economic development.[3]

I

Every schoolchild is taught that Robert Fulton was the first American to build and operate a steamboat on New York waters. When his *Clermont* sauntered four miles per hour upstream on the Hudson River in 1807, Fulton opened up new possibilities in transportation, marketing, and city building. What is not often taught about Fulton is that he had a monopoly enforced by the state. The New York legislature gave Fulton the privilege of carrying *all* steamboat traffic in New York for thirty years.[4] It was this monopoly that Thomas Gibbons, a New Jersey steamboat man, tried to crack when he hired young Cornelius Vanderbilt in 1817 to run steamboats in New York by charging less than the monopoly rates.[5]

Vanderbilt was a classic market entrepreneur, and he was intrigued by the challenge of breaking the Fulton monopoly. On the mast of Gibbon's ship Vanderbilt hoisted a flag that read: "New Jersey must be free." For sixty days in 1817, Vanderbilt defied capture as he raced passengers cheaply from Elizabeth, New Jersey, to New York City. He became a popular figure on the Atlantic as he lowered the fares and eluded the law. Finally, in 1824, in the landmark case of *Gibbons v. Ogden*, the Supreme Court struck down the Fulton monopoly. Chief Justice John Marshall ruled that only the federal government, not the states, could regulate interstate commerce. This extremely popular decision opened the waters of America to complete competition. A jubilant Vanderbilt was greeted in New Brunswick, New Jersey, by cannon salutes fired by "citizens desirous of testifying in a public manner their good will." Ecstatic New Yorkers immediately launched two steamboats named for John Marshall. On the Ohio River, steamboat traffic doubled in the first year after *Gibbons v. Ogden* and quadrupled after the second year.[6]

The triumph of market entrepreneurs in steamboating led to improvements in technology. As one man observed, "The boat builders, freed from the domination of the Fulton-Livingston interests, were quick to develop new ideas that before had no encouragement from capital." These new ideas included tubular boilers to replace the heavy and expensive copper boilers Fulton used. Cordwood for fuel was also a major cost for Fulton, but innovators soon found that anthracite coal worked well under the new tubular boilers, so "the expense of fuel was cut down one-half."[7]

The real value of removing the Fulton monopoly was that the costs of steamboating dropped. Passenger traffic, for example, from New York City to Albany immediately dropped from seven to three dollars after *Gibbons v. Ogden*. Fulton's group couldn't meet the new rates and soon went bankrupt. Gibbons and Vanderbilt, meanwhile, adopted the new technology, cut their costs, and earned $40,000 profit each year during the late 1820s.[8]

With such an open environment for market entrepreneurs, Vanderbilt decided to quit his pleasant association with Gibbons, buy two steamboats, and go into business for himself. During the 1830s, Vanderbilt would establish trade routes all over the northeast. He offered fast and reliable service at low rates. He first tried the New York to Philadelphia route and forced the "standard" three-dollar fare down to one dollar. On the New Brunswick to New York City run, Vanderbilt charged six cents a trip and provided free meals. As *Niles' Register* said, the "times must be hard indeed when a traveller who wishes to save money cannot afford to walk."[9]

Moving to New York, Vanderbilt decided to compete against the Hudson River Steamboat Association, whose ten ships probably made it the largest steamboat line in America in 1830. It tried to informally fix prices to guarantee regular profits. Vanderbilt challenged it with two boats (which he called the "People's Line") and cut the standard New York to Albany fare from three dollars to one dollar, then to ten cents, and finally to nothing. He figured it cost him $200 per day to operate his boats; if he could fill them with 100 passengers, he could take them free if they would each eat and drink two dollars worth of food (Vanderbilt later helped to invent the potato chip). Even if his passengers didn't eat that much, he was putting enormous pressure on his wealthier competitors. Finally, the exasperated Steamboat Association literally bought Vanderbilt out: they gave him $100,000 plus $5,000 a year for ten years if he would promise to leave the Hudson River for the next ten years. Vanderbilt accepted, and the Association raised the Albany fare back to three dollars. Such bribery may be wrong in theory, but it had little effect in practice. With no barriers to entry, other steamboaters came along and quickly cut the fare. They saw that it could be done for less, and they saw what had happened to Vanderbilt for doing it. So almost immediately

The Bettmann Archive — The Bettmann Archive

Robert Fulton (left) and Edward K. Collins. Political entrepreneurs, they were defeated by Vanderbilt's market innovations.

Daniel Drew began running steamboats on the Hudson—until the Association paid him off, too. At least five other competitors did the same thing until they, too, were bought off. It's hard to figure who got the better deal: those who ran the steamboats and were bought out, or those who traveled the steamboats at the new low rates.[10]

Meanwhile, Vanderbilt took his payoff money and bought bigger and faster ships to trim the fares on New England routes. He started with the New York City to Hartford trip and slashed the five-dollar fare to one dollar. He then knocked the New York City to Providence fare in half from eight to four dollars. When he sliced it to one dollar, the New York *Evening Post* called him "the greatest practical anti-monopolist in the country." In these rate wars, sometimes Vanderbilt's competitors bought him out, sometimes they went broke, and sometimes they matched his rates and kept going. Some people denounced Vanderbilt for engaging in extortion, blackmail, and cut-throat competition. Today, of course, he would be found "in restraint of trade" by the Sherman Anti-trust Act. Nonetheless, Vanderbilt qualifies as a market entrepreneur: he fought monopolies, he improved steamship technology, and he cut costs. *Harper's Weekly* insisted that Vanderbilt's actions "must be judged by the results; and the results, in every case, of the establishment of opposition lines by Vanderbilt has been the *permanent reduction of fares.*" The editor went on to say, "Wherever [Vanderbilt] 'laid on' an opposition line, the fares were instantly reduced; and however the contest terminated, whether he bought out his opponents, as he often did, or they bought him out, the fares were never again raised to the old standards." Vanderbilt himself later put it bluntly when he said: "If I could not run a steamship alongside of another man and do it as well as he for twenty percent less than it cost him I would leave the ship."[11]

II

In the 1840s, improving technology changed steamboats into steamships. Larger engines and economies of scale in shipbuilding led to changes in size, speed, and comfort. The new steamers of the mid-century were many times bigger and faster than Fulton's *Clermont*: they were each two decks high with a grand saloon and individual staterooms for first-class passengers. When full, some of these new steamships could hold almost 1,000 passengers, and they also had space for mail and freight. These ships were sturdy and were built to cross the Atlantic Ocean. The New York to England route would be the first to open up the steamship competition; the New York to California line (via Panama) would soon follow.[12] Rapid overseas trade was a new concept, and this reopened the debate for federal aid to eager steamboat operators. Fulton was gone, but others like him argued for government subsidies and contracts. Political and market entrepreneurs on both sides of the Atlantic would fight for control of the seas.

Actually, Englishmen, in 1838, were the first to travel the Atlantic Ocean entirely by steam. The open environment was quickly altered when Samuel Cunard, a political entrepreneur, convinced the English government to give him $275,000 a year to run a semi-monthly mail and passenger service across the ocean. Cunard charged $200 per passenger and $.24 a letter; the $.24 for the mail didn't cover the cost of Cunard's shipping, and that's one argument he had for a subsidy. He also contended that subsidized steamships gave England an advantage in world trade and were a readily available merchant marine in case of war. Parliament accepted this argument and increased government aid to the Cunard line throughout the 1840s.[13]

Soon, political entrepreneurs across the ocean began using these same arguments for federal aid to the new American steamship industry. They argued that America needed subsidized steamships to compete with England to provide a military fleet in case of war. Edward K. Collins, a classic political entrepreneur, exploited these arguments with a self-serving plan. If the government would give him $3,000,000 down and $385,000 a year, he would build five ships and outrace the Cunarders from coast to coast. Collins would deliver the mail, too; and the Americans would get to "drive the Cunarders off the seas." Collins appealed to American nationalism, not to economic efficiency. Americans would not be opening up new lines of communication because the Cunarders had already opened them. Americans would not be delivering mail more often because the Collins's ships, like Cunard's, would sail only every two weeks. Finally, Americans would not be bringing the mail cheaper because the Cunarders could do it for much less.[14]

Once the Senate established the principle of mail subsidy, other political entrepreneurs asked for subsidies to bring the mail to other places. Soon Congress also gave $500,000 a year for two lines to bring mail to California: an Atlantic line to get mail to Panama and a Pacific line to take letters from Panama to California. As in the case of Cunard, Collins and the California operators, all argued that a generous subsidy now would help them become more efficient and lead to no subsidy later.[15]

Congress gave money to the Collins and California lines in 1847, but they took years to build their luxurious ships. Collins, especially, had champagne tastes with taxpayers' money. He built four enormous ships (not five smaller ships as he had promised), each with elegant saloons, ladies' drawing rooms, and wedding berths. He covered the ships with plush carpet and brought aboard rose, satin, and olive-wood furniture, marble tables, exotic mirrors, flexible barber chairs, and French chefs. The state rooms had painted glass windows and electric bells to call the stewards. Collins stressed luxury, not economy, and his ships used almost twice the coal of the Cunard line. He often beat the Cunarders across the ocean by one day (ten days to eleven), but his costs were high and his economic benefits were nil.[16]

With annual government aid, Collins had no incentive to reduce his costs from year to year. His expenses, in fact, more than doubled in 1852: Collins preferred to compete in the world of politics for more federal aid than in the world of business against price-cutting rivals. So in 1852 he went to Washington and lavishly dined and entertained

President Fillmore, his cabinet, and influential Congressmen. Collins artfully lobbied in Congress for an increase to $858,000 a year (or $33,000 each for twenty-six voyages—which came to $5.00 per ocean mile) to compete with the Cunarders.[17]

Meanwhile, Vanderbilt had watched this political entrepreneurship long enough. In 1855 he declared his willingness to deliver the mail for less than Cunard, and for less than half of what Collins was getting. Collins apparently begged Vanderbilt not to go to Congress. He may have offered to help Vanderbilt get an equally large subsidy from Congress—if only he wouldn't open the transatlantic steamship trade. But Vanderbilt had told Collins and Congress that he would run an Atlantic ferry for $15,000 per trip, which was cheaper than anyone else could do.[18]

So in 1855, Collins, the subsidized lobbyist, began battle with Vanderbilt, the market entrepreneur. Collins fought the first round in Congress rather than on the sea. Most Congressmen, former Whigs especially, backed Collins. To do otherwise would be to admit they had made a mistake in helping him earlier; and this might call into question all federal aid. Other Congressmen, especially the New Englanders, had constituents who benefitted from Collins' business. Senator William Seward of New York stressed another angle by asking, "Could you accept that proposition of Vanderbilt['s] justly, without, at the same time, taking the Collins steamers and paying for them?" In other words, Seward is saying that we backed Collins at the start, now we are committed to him, so let's support him no matter what. Vanderbilt, by contrast, warned that "private enterprise may be driven from any of the legitimate channels of commerce by means of bounties." His point was that it is hard for unsubsidized ships to compete with subsidized ships for mail and passengers. Since the contest is unfair from the start, the subsidized ships have a potential monopoly of all trade. But Collins' lobbying prevailed, so Congress turned Vanderbilt down and kept payments to Collins at $858,000 per year.[19]

Vanderbilt decided to challenge Collins even without a subsidy. "The share of prosperity which has fallen to my lot," said Vanderbilt, "is the direct result of unfettered trade, and unrestrained competition. It is my wish that those who are to come after me shall have that same field open before them." Vanderbilt's strategy against Collins was to charge only $.15 for half-ounce letters and to cut the standard first-class fare $20, to $110. Later he slashed it to $80. Van-

The Bettmann Archive

The Monitor and the Merrimac. Vanderbilt offered to personally sink the Confederate ship Merrimac, asking only that everyone "stay out of the way when I am hunting the critter."

derbilt also introduced a new service: a cheaper third-class fare in the steerage. The steerage must have been uncomfortable—people were practically stacked on top of each other—but for $75, and sometimes less, he did get newcomers to travel.[20]

To beat the subsidized Collins, Vanderbilt found creative ways to cut expenses. First, he had little or no insurance on his fleet. He always said that if insurance companies could make money on shipping, so could he. So Vanderbilt built his ships well, hired excellent captains, and saved money on insurance. Second, he spent less than Collins did for repairs and maintenance. Collins' ships cost more than Vanderbilt's, but they were not seaworthy. The engines were too big for the hulls, so the ships vibrated and sometimes leaked. They usually needed days of repairing after each trip. Third, Collins, like Cunard in England, was elitist with his government aid. He cared little for cheap passenger traffic. Vanderbilt, by contrast hired local "runners," who buttonholed all kinds of people to travel on his ships. These second- and third-class passengers were important because all steamship operators had fixed costs for making each voyage. They had to pay a set amount for coal, crew, maintenance, food, and docking fees. In such a situation, Vanderbilt needed volume business. With third-class fares, Vanderbilt sometimes carried over 500 passengers per ship.

Even so, Vanderbilt barely survived the first year competing against Collins. He complained, "It is utterly impossible for a private individual to stand in competition with a line drawing nearly one million dollars per annum from the national treasury, without serious sacrifice." He added that such aid was "inconsistent with the. . .economy and prudence essential to the successful management of any private enterprise."[21]

Vanderbilt met this challenge by spending $600,000 building a new steamship, immodestly named the *Vanderbilt*, "the largest vessel which has ever floated on the Atlantic Ocean." The Commodore built the ship with a beam engine, which was more powerful than Collins' traditional side-lever engines. In a head-to-head race, the *Vanderbilt* beat Collins' ship to England and won the Blue Ribbon, an award given to the one ship owning the fastest time from New York City to Liverpool. By 1856, Collins had two ships—half of his accident-prone fleet—sink (killing almost 500 passengers). In desperation, he spent over a million dollars of government money building a gigantic replacement; but he built it so poorly that it could make only two trips and had to be sold at more than a $900,000 loss.[22]

Even Collins' friends in Congress could defend him no longer. Between Collins' obvious mismanagement and Vanderbilt's unsubsidized trips, most Congressmen soured on federal subsidies. Senator Judah P. Benjamin of Louisiana said, "I believe [the Collins line] has been most miserably managed." Senator Robert M. T. Hunter of Virginia went further: "the whole system was wrong;. . .it ought to have been left, like any other trade, to competition." Senator John B. Thompson of Kentucky said, "Give neither this line, nor any other line, a subsidy. . . . Let the Collins line die. . . . I want a tabula rasa—the whole thing wiped out, and a new beginning." Congress voted for this "new beginning" in 1858: they revoked Collins' aid and left him to compete with Vanderbilt on an equal basis. The results: Collins quickly went bankrupt, and Vanderbilt became the leading American steamship operator.[23]

And there was yet another twist. When Vanderbilt competed against the English, his major competition did not come from the Cunarders. The new unsubsidized William Inman Line was doing to Cunard in England what Vanderbilt had done to Collins in America. The subsidized Cunard had cautiously stuck with traditional technology, while William Inman had gone on to use screw propellers and iron hulls instead of paddle wheels and wood. It worked; and from 1858 to the Civil War, two market entrepreneurs, Vanderbilt and Inman, led America and England in cheap mail and passenger service.[24]

The mail subsidies, then, actually retarded progress because Cunard and Collins both used their monopolies to stifle innovation and delay technological changes in steamship construction. Several English steamship companies experimented with iron hulls and screw propellers in the 1840s, but Cunard thwarted this whenever he could. According to Royal Meeker,

> The mail payments made it possible for the Cunard company to cling to an out-of-date and uneconomical type of steamer. Both the Admiralty and the Post Office departments refused to permit mail steamers to use the screw propeller until long after other lines had adopted it. . . . Without government aid to inefficiency, the Cunard Company would have been compelled to adopt improvements in order to compete with other and more progressive lines.

Cunard also refused to introduce a third-class rate. So, when William Inman came along in the 1850s with his iron ships and third-class fares, he practically knocked Cunard out of business. After 1850, Inman and other newcomers kept the pressure on Cunard. They experimented with oscillating cabins (to reduce the impact of the swaying of the ship), compound engines (to increase the ship's speed and decrease its fuel consumption), and twin propellers. Cunard's subsidy kept him from having to innovate and protected him from errors of judgment that would have ruined his competitors.[25]

In America, Collins, like Cunard, chose wood and paddle wheels for his ships. Americans were slower to turn to iron ships because their costs of iron construction were higher than those in England. Still, American engineers had been experimenting with iron hulls and screw propellers during the 1840s, partly because iron was more durable in handling the big engines built after 1840. Collins apparently considered using iron, but he was no innovator. So he ended up using wood hulls for his powerful engines, and his ships were not as safe or as seaworthy because of that. With Collins using wood, American steamship operators feared switching to iron. They had little margin for error because their chief competitor was subsidized. Yet in 1851, Vanderbilt became one of the first Americans to build and run iron ships (he used them on his California route). But it wasn't until Collins' subsidy expired in 1858 that Americans began experimenting with iron hulls in a serious way.[26]

This delay in experimenting with iron meant that iron ships could not be much of a force during the Civil War. John Ericsson, who in 1862 built the iron-hulled *Monitor*, had been promoting the advantages of iron ships since 1843. But in 1847, when Collins decided to use wood for his subsidized fleet, only Vanderbilt dared to risk more experiments with iron hulls. The irony here is that one of the central arguments for subsidizing Collins was that his fleet would be usable in case of war. Yet his outmoded wooden ships—even the ones that didn't sink—would have been helpless against ironclad opponents. And we wouldn't have needed them anyway because Vanderbilt gave his 5,000-ton ship, the *Vanderbilt*, as a permanent gift to the United States during the Civil War. He even offered to personally sink the Confederate's *Merrimac*, asking only that everyone stay "out of the way when I am hunting the critter." He never got the chance; and, partly because of the Collins subsidy, the U.S.

never got the chance to blockade Confederate ports with an iron fleet. Who knows whether or not that would have shortened the war? It certainly would have relieved those who feared that the Confederates would buy iron ships from England. And it would have relieved the Secretary of War, Edwin Stanton, who worried that the *Merrimac* would go on a rampage, sail up the Potomac unmolested, and blow the dome off the Capitol.[27]

III

Vanderbilt was also cast as a market entrepreneur in his battle for the steamship traffic to California. Two California lines—the U.S. Mail Steamship Company and the Pacific Mail Steamship Company—started mail delivery in 1849 with $500,000 per year in federal aid. As happened with Collins, these mail contracts were not opened for bidding; they were a private deal between the Post Office and the two steamship companies. At first the two lines charged company rates: $600 per passenger from New York to California, via railroad over Panama. As the gold-rush traffic increased, Vanderbilt became convinced that more gold could be made in steamships than in the hills of California—even without a subsidy. Vanderbilt chose not to challenge the subsidized lines directly through Panama; instead he built a canal through Nicaragua. It took Vanderbilt a year to deepen and clean out the San Juan River in Nicaragua, but it was worth it because the Nicaraguan route was 500 miles shorter to California. So Vanderbilt agreed to pay the Nicaraguan government $10,000 a year for canal privileges. He then slashed the California fare to $400 and promised all passengers that he would beat the rival steamships to the gold fields. He even offered to carry the mail free. After a year of rate-cutting the fare dropped to $150; yet Vanderbilt and his competitors apparently were still making money.[28]

Such a development tells us a lot about the subsidy system. The California lines originally got a half-million dollars a year from the government; then they charged people $600 to get to California. Yet Vanderbilt, with no outside aid, ran a profitable line to California by charging passengers only $150 and carrying the mail free. He hoped that doing this would expose his subsidized opponents and end their federal aid. But the California lines, like Collins, artfully pleaded to Congress for a subsidy even larger (which they needed to beat Vanderbilt). And they got $900,000 a year to compete with the more efficient Vanderbilt.[29]

In the next stage of the subsidy saga, Vanderbilt had his canal rights revoked by the Nicaraguan government in 1854. Behind this movement was William Walker, an American with a bizarre mission. Walker shipped a small army into Nicaragua, overthrew the existing government, proclaimed himself the president and revoked Vanderbilt's canal rights. Since Vanderbilt's canal company was chartered in Nicaragua, the American government was technically not obligated to help him. So the enraged Vanderbilt put his ships on the Panama route, instead. There he competed head to head against the California mail carriers. He then cut the fare to $100 ($30 for third class) and swore he would beat the subsidized California lines and any new line in Nicaragua that Walker might help establish.[30]

The operators of the California lines were typical political entrepreneurs: they did not want to compete with a market entrepreneur like Vanderbilt. So they bought him out instead by paying him most of their subsidy if he promised not to run any ships to California. Vanderbilt demanded and received $672,000, or 75 percent, of the $900,000 annual subsidy. But more than this, he wanted his Nicaragua canal back. So he dabbled in Central American politics and helped get Walker overthrown. Unfortunately for Vanderbilt, his canal had been permanently destroyed during Walker's coup; but since he had the pay-off money from the California lines, he ended up with a profit anyway.[31]

Congress was astonished when it learned what the California lines were doing with their $900,000 subsidy. In 1858 Senator Robert A. Toombs of Georgia said that he admired Vanderbilt: his "superior skills," Toombs said, had exposed the whole subsidy system. "You give $900,000 a year to carry the mails to California; and Vanderbilt compels the contractors to give him $56,000 a month to keep quiet. This is the effect of your subventions. . . . [Vanderbilt] is the kingfish that is robbing these small plunderers that come about the Capitol. He does not come here for that purpose." Toombs' conclusion: end the mail subsidies.[32]

Many people, though, were more critical of Vanderbilt than of the subsidies. They looked at Vanderbilt's tactics, instead of his influence on the market. One court later called Vanderbilt's actions "immoral and in restraint of trade." The *New York Times* compared Vanderbilt to "those old German barons who, from their eyries along the Rhine, swooped down upon the commerce of the noble river, and wrung tribute from every passenger that floated by."[33] From Vanderbilt's standpoint, the California lines were the ones "in restraint of trade." Their subsidies gave them an unfair advantage over all competition, and they used this advantage to charge monopoly rates to passengers. As for the "swooping" metaphor, Vanderbilt "swooped down" and " wrung tribute" from the subsidized lines, not from "every passenger." Every passenger, in fact, paid lower fares to California because Vanderbilt's competition had slashed the fares permanently.[34] And, of course, if there had been no government subsidy, there would have been no Vanderbilt payoff. Vanderbilt ran his California lines as a personal investment and charged passengers less than one-fourth the fare that the subsidized lines had been charging. Congress, however, had committed its support for political entrepreneurs. And the annual $900,000 subsidy proved to be so large that the California lines could give three-fourths of it to Vanderbilt and still make money. Without Vanderbilt, this political entrepreneurship might have gone on much longer.

This clash between market and political entrepreneurs changed the competitive environment of American steamboating. Between 1848 and 1858, the American government paid the two California lines and Edward Collins over eleven million dollars to build ships and carry mail. Vanderbilt, by contrast, engaged these men in head-to-head competition free of charge. Largely because of Vanderbilt, Congress, in 1858, ended all mail subsidies. Afterward, Vanderbilt and others carried the mail only for the postage; and the passenger rates after 1858 were still competitive: only $200 to California, far below the original monopoly rate of $600.[35]

Vanderbilt's victory marked the end of political entrepreneurship in the American steamship business. We didn't end up with perfect free trade, but we were closer to it than we ever had been. In this environment, Americans found railroads to be more profitable investments than steamships. So, after the Civil War, Vanderbilt and others sold their fleets and spent their money building railroads. The percentage of American exports carried on American ships dropped from sixty-seven to nine percent from 1860 to 1915, but that was no problem. England's comparative advantage in shipping lowered America's cost for freight, mail, and passenger service throughout these years. And since the English were anxious to buy America's grain, Vanderbilt took his steamship profits and built his New York Central Railroad over one thousand miles out to Chicago and other midwestern cities. When Vanderbilt shipped midwestern grain to

New York and had it boarded on English ships to be sold in Liverpool, both countries were finally doing what they could do best. By Vanderbilt's death in 1877, he had been a central figure in America's industrial revolution, both in steam and in rails. He also was worth almost $100 million, which made him the richest man in America.[36]

This study of American steamboating focuses on the market and the impact different entrepreneurs had on the market. If we look at the issue this way, we can sort out two distinct groups: political and market entrepreneurs. Robert Fulton, Edward Collins, and Samuel Cunard cannot be lumped with Thomas Gibbons, Cornelius Vanderbilt, and William Inman. They are two separate groups with different attitudes toward innovation, technology, price-cutting, monopolies, and federal aid. In the steamship industry, political entrepreneurship often led to price-fixing, technological stagnation, and the bribing of competitors and politicians. The market entrepreneurs were the innovators and rate-cutters. They said they had to be to survive against subsidized opponents. Some of them were personally repugnant (Vanderbilt disinherited his son and placed his own wife in an asylum; Gibbons tried to horsewhip one of his rivals), but they advanced their industry and cut passenger fares permanently. Since Vanderbilt ended up as the richest man in America, perhaps the federal aid was a curse, not a blessing, even to those who received it.

"Making a difference in the way the world worked"

Courtesy James J. Hill Reference Library

James J. Hill, age 25

CHAPTER TWO

James J. Hill and the Transcontinental Railroads

The story of the building of the transcontinental railroads makes for good reading. It has a sound plot: four railroads get charters and subsidies to build across the country. It has suspense: the Union Pacific and Central Pacific frantically race across plains and over mountains to complete the railroad. It has an all-star cast: U.S. Presidents, army generals, and political adventurers confront Indians on the warpath, politicians on the take, and thousands of Chinese and Irish workers. The story tells of the agony of defeat—Indian raids and winter storms—and the thrill of victory with the meeting of the Union and Central Pacific in Utah and the final hammering of the golden spike. Finally, there is celebrating as the story ends: Western Union telegraphs the event across the nation, and revelers sound the Liberty Bell from Independence Hall.

Over the years historians have told this story and described the drama, but they have often criticized the main actors and their exploits. The grab for federal subsidies seems to have led to greed and corruption; but—and this is the key point—most historians say there was no way to get the happy ending to the transcontinental story without federal aid. "Unless the government had been willing to build the transcontinental lines itself," John Garraty typically asserts, "some system of subsidy was essential."[1]

But there is a nagging problem in this argument. While some of this rush for subsidies was still going on, James J. Hill was building a transcontinental from St. Paul to Seattle with no federal aid whatsoever. Also, Hill's road was the best built, the least corrupt, the most popular, and the only transcontinental never to go bankrupt. It took longer to build than the others, but Hill used this time to get the shortest route on the best grade with the least curvature. In doing so, he attracted settlement and trade by cutting costs for passengers and freight. Could it be that, in the long run, the subsidies may have corrupted railroad development and hindered economic growth? The transcontinental story is worth a more careful look. It may have a different ending if we move Hill from a cameo role to that of a leading actor.

The dream of a transcontinental had excited promoters and patriots ever since the Mexican War and the acquisition of California. Congress spent $150,000 during the 1850s surveying three possible routes from the Mississippi River to the west coast. In 1862, with the Southern Democrats out of the union, Congress hastily passed the Pacific Railroad Act. This act led to the creating of the Union Pacific, which would lay rails west from Omaha, and the Central Pacific, which would start in Sacramento and build east. Since congressmen wanted the road built quickly, they did two key things. First, they gave each line twenty alternate sections of land for each mile of track completed. Second, they gave loans: $16,000 for each mile of track of flat prairie land, $32,000 per mile for hilly terrain, and $48,000 per mile in the mountains.[2]

The UP and CP, then, would compete for government largess. The line that built the most miles would get the most cash and land. The land, of course, would be sold; and this way the railroad would be financed. In this arrangement, the incentive was for speed, not efficiency. The two lines spent little time choosing routes; they just laid track and cashed in.

The subsidies shaped the UP builders' strategy in the following ways. They moved west from Omaha in 1865 along the Platte River. Since they were being paid by the mile, they sometimes built winding, circuitous roads to collect for more mileage. For construction they used cheap and light wrought iron rails, soon to be outmoded by Bessemer rails. And Thomas Durant, vice-president and general manager, stressed speed, not workmanship. "You are doing too much in masonry this year," Durant told a staff member; "substitute tressel [sic] and wooden culverts for masonry wherever you can for the present." Also, since trees were scarce on the plains, Durant and his chief engineer, Grenville Dodge, were hard pressed to make railroad ties, 2300 of which were needed to finish each mile of track. Sometimes they shipped in wood; other times they used the fragile cottonwood found in the Platte River Valley; often, though, they artfully solved their problem by passing it on to others. The UP simply paid top wages to tie-cutters and daily bonuses for ties received. Hordes of tie-cutters, therefore, invaded Nebraska, cut trees wherever they were found, and delivered freshly cut ties right up to the UP line. The UP leaders conveniently argued that, since most of Nebraska was unsurveyed, farmers in the way were therefore squatters and held no right to any trees on this "public land." Some farmers used rifles to defend their land; and, in the wake of violence, even Durant discovered "that it was not good policy to take all the timber."[3]

The rush for subsidies caused other building problems, too. Nebraska winters were long and hard; but, since Dodge was in a hurry, he laid track on the ice and snow anyway. Naturally the line had to be rebuilt in the spring. What was worse, unanticipated spring flooding along the Loup fork of the Platte River washed out rails, bridges, and telephone poles, doing at least $50,000 damage the first year. No wonder some observers estimated the actual building cost at almost three times what it should have been.[4]

By pushing rail lines through unsettled land, the transcontinentals invited Indian attacks, which caused the loss of hundreds of lives and further ran up the cost of building. The Cheyenne and Sioux harassed the road throughout Nebraska and Wyoming: they stole horses, damaged track, and scalped workmen along the way. The government paid the costs of sending extra troops along the line to help protect it. But when they left, the graders, tie-setters, tracklayers, and bolters often had to work in teams with half of them standing guard and the other half working. In some cases, such as the Plum Creek massacre in Nebraska, the UP attorney admitted his line was negligent: it had sent workingmen into areas known to be frequented by hostile Indians.[5]

As the UP and CP entered Utah in 1869, the competition became fiercer and more costly. Both sides graded lines that paralleled each other and both claimed subsidies for this mileage. As they approached each other the workers on the UP, mostly Irish, assaulted those on the CP, mostly Chinese. In a series of attacks and counterattacks, with boulders and gunpowder, many lives were lost and much track was destroyed. Both sides involved Presidents Johnson and Grant in the feuding. With the threat of a federal investigation looming, the two lines finally compromised on Promontory Point,

Utah, as their meeting place. There they joined tracks on May 10, with hoopla, speeches, and the veneer of unity. After the celebration, however, both of the shoddily constructed lines had to be rebuilt and sometimes relocated, a task that the UP didn't finish until five years later. As Dodge said one week before the historic meeting, "I never saw so much needless waste in building railroads. Our own construction department has been inefficient."[6]

After the construction was completed, many were astonished at the costs of construction. The UP and CP, even with 44,000,000 acres of free land and over $61,000,000 in cash loans, were almost bankrupt. Two other circumstances helped to keep costs high. First, the costs of building a railroad, or anything else for that matter, were abnormally high after the Civil War. Capital and labor were scarce; also, even without the harsh winters and the Indians, it was costly to feed thousands of workmen who were sometimes hundreds of miles from a nearby town. Second, the officers of the Union and Central Pacific created their own supply companies and bought materials for their roads from these companies. The UP, for example, needed coal, so six of its officers created the Wyoming Coal and Mining Company. They mined coal for $2.00 per ton (later reduced to $1.10) and sold it to the UP for as high as $6.00 a ton. Even more significant, the Credit Mobilier, which was also run by UP officials, supplied iron and other materials to the UP at exorbitant prices. What they didn't make running the railroad, they made selling to the railroad.[7]

Many people then and now have pointed accusing fingers at the UP with its Credit Mobilier and its wasteful building. But this misdirects the problem. If we look at the subsidies instead, we can see that they dictated the building strategy and dramatically shaped the outcome. Granted, the leaders of the UP were greedy and showed poor judgment. But the presence of free land and cash tempted them to rush west, then made them dependent on federal aid to survive.

No wonder the UP courted politicians so carefully. In this arrangement they were more precious than freight or passengers. In 1866, Thomas Durant wined and dined 150 "prominent citizens" (including Senators, an ambassador, and government bureaucrats) along a completed section of the railroad. He hired an orchestra, a caterer, six cooks, a magician (to pull subsidies out of a hat?), and a photographer. For those with ecumenical palates, he served Chinese duck and Roman goose; the more adventurous were offered roast ox and antelope. All could have expensive wine and, for dessert, strawberries, peaches, and cherries. After dinner some of the men hunted buffalo from their coaches. Durant hoped that all would go back to Washington inclined to repay the UP for its hospitality. If not, the UP could appeal to a man's wallet as well as his stomach. In Congress and in state legislatures, free railroad passes were distributed like confetti. For a more personal touch, the UP let General William T. Sherman buy a section of its land near Omaha for $2.50 an acre when the going rate was $8.00. In case that failed, Oakes Ames, president of the UP, handed out Credit Mobilier stock to congressmen at a discount "where it would do the most good." It was for this act, not for selling the UP overpriced goods, that Congress censured Oakes Ames and then investigated the UP line.[8]

The airing of the Credit Mobilier scandal—just four years after the celebrating at Promontory Point—soured many voters on the UP. Others were annoyed because the UP was so inefficient that it couldn't pay back any of its borrowed money. Just as the UP was birthed and nurtured on federal aid, though, so it would have to mature on federal supervision and regulation.

In 1874, Congress passed the Thurman Law, which forced the UP to pay 25 percent of its net earnings each year into a sinking fund to retire its federal debt. Because the line was so badly put together, it competed poorly and needed the sinking fund money to stay afloat. Building branch lines to get rural traffic would have helped the UP, but the government often wouldn't give them permission. President Sidney Dillon called his line "an apple tree without a limb," and concluded, "unless we have branches there will be no fruit." Congress further squashed any trace of ingenuity or independence by passing a law creating a Bureau of Railroad Accounts to investigate the UP books regularly. Of these federal restrictions, Charles Francis Adams, Jr., a later president, complained: "We cannot lease; we cannot guarantee, and we cannot make new loans on business principles, for we cannot mortgage or pledge; we cannot build extensions, we cannot contract loans as other people contract them. All these things are [prohibited] to us; yet all these things are habitually done by our competitors." The power to subsidize, Adams discovered, was the power to destroy.

John M. Thurston, the UP's solicitor general, saw this connection between government aid and government control. The UP, he said, was "perhaps more at the mercy of adverse legislation than any other corporation in the United States, by reason of its Congressional charter and its indebtedness to the government and the power of Congress over it."[9]

When Jay Gould took control of the UP in 1874, his solution was to use and create monopoly advantages to raise prices, fatten profits, and cancel debts. For example, he paid the Pacific Mail Steamship Company not to compete with the UP along the west coast. Then he raised rates 40 to 100 percent and, a few weeks later, hiked them another 20 to 33 percent. This allowed him to pay off some debts and even declare a rare stock dividend; but it soon brought more consumer wrath, and this translated into more government regulation and, eventually, helped lead to the Interstate Commerce Commission, which outlawed rate discrimination.[10]

It is sad to read of the UP struggling for survival in the 1870s and 1880s, only to collapse into bankruptcy in 1893. Yet it's hard to see how its history could have taken any other direction, given the presence of government aid. The aid bred inefficiency; the inefficiency created consumer wrath; the consumer wrath led to government regulation; and the regulation closed the UP's options and helped lead to bankruptcy.

The Central Pacific did better, but only because its circumstances were different. Its leaders—Leland Stanford, Collis Huntington, Charles Crocker, and Mark Hopkins—were united on narrow goals and worked together effectively to achieve them. These men, the "Big Four," focused mainly on one state, California, and used their wealth and political pull to dominate (and sometimes bribe) California legislators. Stanford, who was elected Governor and U.S. Senator, controlled politics for the Big Four and prevented any competing railroad from entering California. Profits from the resulting monopoly rates were added to windfall gains from their Contract and Finance Company, which was the counterpart of the Credit Mobilier. Unlike the UP leaders in the Credit Mobilier scandal, the Big Four escaped jail because the records of the Contract and Finance Company "accidentally" were destroyed. Without records, it was left to Frank Norris to tell the story of the CP monopoly in his novel, *The Octopus*. It was almost 1900 before privately funded railroads could muster the financial strength and the political muscle to take on the entrenched CP (later renamed the Southern Pacific) in California politics.[11]

In case Congress needed another lesson, the story of the Northern Pacific again featured government subsidies. Congressmen chartered the Northern Pacific in 1864 as a transcontinental running through the Northwest. They gave it no loans, but granted it forty sections of land per mile, which was twice what the UP received. Various owners floundered and even bankrupted the NP, until Henry Villard took control in 1881. Villard had come to America at age eighteen from Bavaria in 1853. Shortly after he arrived, he showed a flair for journalism; he won recognition for his writing during the Civil War. In his writing and in his speaking, Villard developed the ability to persuade others to follow him. He first became interested in the Northwest in 1874; he was hired as an agent for German bondholders in America and went to Oregon to analyze their investments. He liked what he saw and began to have grandiose visions about a transportation empire in the Northwest. He soon began buying NP stock and took charge of the stagnant railroad in 1881.[12]

Villard had many of the traits of his fellow transcontinental operators. First, like Jay Gould, he manipulated stock; in fact, he bought his NP shares on margin and used overcapitalized stock as collateral for his margin account. Second, like the Big Four on the CP, Villard liked monopolies. He even bought railroads and steamships along the Pacific coast, not for their value, but to remove them as competitors. Finally, like the leaders of the UP, Villard eagerly sought the 44,000,000 acres the government had promised him for building a railroad.

Villard's strategy, then, resembled that of the other builders. He had an added plus, though, in his skills in promoting and coaxing funds from wealthy investors. "I feel absolutely confident," he wrote, "that we shall be able to work results. . .that will astonish every participant." Hundreds of German investors, and others too, heeded the call for funds and sent Villard $8,000,000 to bring the NP to the west coast. Businessmen everywhere were amazed at Villard's persuasive ways. "This is the greatest feat of strategy I ever performed," Villard proclaimed, "and I am constantly being congratulated ...upon...the achievement." So with his friends' $8,000,000, and with the government's free land, Villard pushed the NP westward and arrived in Seattle, Washington, in 1883. His celebration, however, was short-lived because that same year the NP almost declared bankruptcy and Villard was ousted.[13]

If we look at Villard's actions, we can see why he failed. First, like the other transcontinental builders, he rushed into the wilderness to collect his subsidies. Villard knew that the absence of settlement

The Bettmann Archive

Leland Stanford (1814–1893): used his political and financial power to prevent competing railroads from entering California.

meant the absence of traffic, but his solution was to promote tourism as well as immigration. He thought tourists would pay to enjoy the beauty of the Northwest, so he built some of the line along a scenic route. This hiked Villard's costs because he had to increase the grade, the curvature, and the length of the railroad to accommodate the Rocky Mountain view. Villard also created some expensive health spas around the hot springs at Bozeman and in Broadwater County, Montana. He also put glass domes around the hot springs and built plush hotels near them to accommodate the throng of tourists he predicted would come. Despite lavish advertising in the east, though, the tourists went elsewhere and Villard went broke.[14]

The federal aid and the foreign investors had given Villard some room for error. But he made other mistakes, too. He was so anxious to rush to the coast that he built when construction costs were high. They were much lower three years before and three years after he built. High costs meant high rates, and this deterred freight and immigrants from traveling along the NP. Villard could have cut some of these costs, but as Julius Grodinsky has observed of Villard, "What was asked, he paid." He didn't bother to learn much about railroads; in fact, during 1883 he seems to have been more interested in leveling six houses in New York City to build a glam-

The Bettmann Archive

Henry Villard (1835–1900): a political entrepreneur who "rushed into the wilderness to collect his subsidies."

orous mansion, in which to entertain the city's elite. With the NP he thought he could promote immigration, tourism, scenic routes, health spas, and use the free land and foreign cash to cover the costs. When his bubble burst, the NP went bankrupt and the German investors were ruined. But not so Villard—from his mansion in New York City, he raised more money and took control of the NP again five years later. The smooth-talking Villard, however, still could not overcome his earlier errors. The poorly constructed Northern Pacific was so inefficient that even the Villard charm could not make it turn a profit. In 1893, the NP went bankrupt again and the Villard era was over.[15]

Villard's failure was pathetic but in some ways understandable. The American Northwest was a tough section for building a railroad. It had a sparse population and a rugged terrain. Oddly enough, though, one man did come along and did build a transcontinental through the Northwest. In fact, he built it north of the NP, almost touching the Canadian border. And he did it with no federal aid. That man was James J. Hill, and his story tells us a lot about the larger problem of federal aid to railroads.

Hill's life could have made good copy for Horatio Alger. He was born in a log cabin in Ontario, Canada, in 1838. His father died when the boy was young, and he supported his mother by working in a grocery for $4.00 per month. He lost use of his right eye in an accident, so his opportunities seemed limited. But Hill was a risk-taker and a doer. At age seventeen he aimed for adventure in the Orient, but settled for a steamer to St. Paul. There he clerked for a shipping company and learned the transportation business. He was good at it and became intrigued with the future of the Northwest.[16]

The American Northwest was America's last frontier. The states from Minnesota to Washington made up one-sixth of the nation, but remained undeveloped for years. The climate was harsh and the terrain was imposing. There were obvious possibilities with the trees, coal, and copper in the region; but crossing it and connecting it with the rest of the nation was formidable. The Rocky Mountains divided the area into distinct parts: to the east were Montana, North Dakota, and Minnesota, which were dry, cold, flat, and, predictably, empty. It was part of what pioneers called "The Great American Desert." Once the Rockies were crossed, the land in Idaho and Washington turned green with forests and plentiful rain. But the road to the coast was broken by the almost uncrossable canyons and jagged peaks of the Cascade Mountains. Since the Northwest was fragmented in geography, remote in location, and harsh in climate, most settlers stopped in the lower Great Plains or went on to California.

To most, the Northwest was, in the words of General William T. Sherman, "as bad [a piece of land] as God ever made." To others, like Villard, the Northwest was a chance to grab some subsidies and create a railroad monopoly. But to Hill the Northwest was an opportunity to develop America's last frontier. Where some saw deserts and mountains, Hill had a vision of farms and cities. Villard might build a few swanky hotels and health spas, but Hill wanted to settle the land and develop the resources. Villard preferred to approach the Northwest from his mansion in New York City. Hill learned the Northwest firsthand, working on the docks in St. Paul, piloting a steamboat on the Red River, and travelling on snowshoes in North Dakota. Villard was attracted to the Northern Pacific because of its monopoly potential; Hill wanted to build a railroad to develop the region, and then to prosper with it.[17]

Hill's years of maturing in St. Paul followed a logical course; from investing in shipping, he switched to steamships, then to railroads. In 1878, he and a group of Canadian friends bought the bankrupt St. Paul and Pacific Railroad from a group of Dutch bondholders.

We don't know whether or not he then had the vision to turn it into a privately financed transcontinental. The St. Paul and Pacific story, like that of the other transcontinentals, had been one of federal subsidies, stock manipulation, profit-taking on construction, and bankruptcy. Its ten miles of track were sometimes unconnected and were made of fifteen separate patterns of iron. Bridge material, ties, and equipment were scattered along the right-of-way. When Hill and his friends bought this railroad and announced their intention to complete it, critics dubbed it "Hill's Folly." Yet he did complete it, ran it profitably, and soon decided to expand it into North Dakota. It was not yet a transcontinental, but it was in the process of becoming one.[18]

As Hill built his railroad across the Northwest, he followed a consistent strategy. First, he always built slowly and developed the export of the area before he moved farther west. In the Great Plains this export was wheat, and Hill promoted dry-farming to increase wheat yields. He advocated diversifying crops and imported 7,000 cattle from England and elsewhere, handing them over free of charge to settlers near his line. Hill was a pump-primer. He knew that if farmers prospered, their freight would give him steady returns every year. The key was to get people to come to the Northwest. To attract immigrants, Hill offered to bring them out to the Northwest for a mere $10.00 each if they would farm near his railroad. "You are now our children," Hill would tell immigrants, "but we are in the same boat with you, and we have got to prosper with you or we have got to be poor with you." To make sure they prospered, he even set up his own experimental farms to test new seed, livestock, and equipment. He promoted crop rotation, mixed farming, and the use of fertilizers. Finally, he sponsored contests and awarded prizes to those who raised meaty livestock or grew abundant wheat.[19]

Unlike Villard, Hill built his railroad for durability and efficiency, not for scenery. "What we want," Hill said, "is the best possible line, shortest distance, lowest grades and least curvature that we can build. We do not care enough for Rocky Mountain scenery to spend a large sum of money developing it." That meant that Hill personally supervised the surveying and the construction. "I find that it pays to be where the money is being spent," noted Hill, but he didn't skimp on quality materials. He believed that building a functional and durable product saved money in the long run. For example, he usually imported high quality Bessemer rails, even though they cost more than those made in America. He was thinking about the future, and quality building cut costs in the long run. When Hill constructed the solid granite Stone Arch Bridge—2100 feet long, 28 feet wide, and 82 feet high—across the Mississippi River it became the Minneapolis landmark for decades.[20]

Hill's quest for short routes, low grades, and few curvatures was an obsession. In 1889, Hill conquered the Rocky Mountains by finding the legendary Marias Pass. Lewis and Clark had described a low pass through the Rockies back in 1805; but later no one seemed to know whether it really existed or, if it did, where it was. Hill wanted the best gradient so much that he hired a man to spend months searching western Montana for this legendary pass. He did in fact find it, and the ecstatic Hill shortened his route almost one hundred miles.[21]

As Hill pushed westward, slowly but surely, the Northern Pacific was there to challenge him. Villard had had first choice of routes, lavish financing from Germany, and 44,000,000 acres of free federal land. Yet it was Hill who was producing the superior product at a competitive cost. His investments in quality rails, low gradients, and short routes saved him costs in repairs and fuel every trip across the Northwest. Hill, for example, was able to outrun the Northern Pacific from coast to coast at least partly because his Great Northern line was 115 miles shorter than Villard's NP.

More than this, though, Hill bested Villard in the day-to-day matters of running a railroad. For example, Villard got his coal from Indiana, but Hill got his from Iowa and saved $2.00 per ton. In the volatile leasing game, Hill outmaneuvered Villard and got a lower cost to the Chicago market. As Hill said, "A railroad is successful in the proportion that its affairs are vigilantly looked after."[22]

Villard may have realized he was outclassed, so he countered with obstructionism, not improved efficiency. One of Hill's partners alerted him to Villard's "egotistic stamp" and concluded that "Villard's vanity will be apt to lead him to reject any treaty of peace that does not seem to gratify his vain desire to obtain a triumph." Before Hill could move out of Minnesota, for example, the NP refused him permission to cross its line at Moorhead, along the Minnesota-North Dakota border. Local citizens apparently wanted Hill's line; and he wrote, "I had a letter from a leading Moorhead merchant today offering 500 good citizen tracklayers to help us at the crossing." Each move west that Hill made threatened Villard's monopoly. Ironically,

Hill sometimes had to use the NP to deliver rails; when he did Villard sometimes raised rates so high that Hill used the Canadian Pacific when he could.[23]

Villard found that manipulating politics was the best way to thwart Hill. For example, the gaining of right-of-way through Indian reservations was a thorny political issue. Legally, no railroad had the right to pass through Indian land. The NP, as a federally funded transcontinental, had a special dispensation. Hill, however, didn't, so the NP and UP tried to block Congress from granting Hill right-of-way through four Indian reservations in North Dakota and Montana. Hill gladly offered to pay the willing Indians fair market value for their land, but Congress stalled, and Hill said, "All our contracts [are] in abeyance until [this] question can be settled." Hill had to fight the NP and UP several times on this issue before getting Congress to grant him his right-of-way. "It really seems hard," Hill later wrote, "when we look back at what we have done in opening the country and carrying at the lowest rates, that we should be compelled to fight political adventurers who have never done anything but pose and draw a salary."[24]

In the depression year of 1893, all the transcontinental owners but Hill were lobbying in Congress for more government loans. To one of them Hill wrote, "The government should not furnish capital to these companies, in addition to their enormous land subsidies, to enable them to conduct their business in competition with enterprises that have received no aid from the public treasury." He proudly concluded, "Our own line in the North. . .was built without any government aid, even the right of way, through hundreds of miles of public lands, being paid for in cash."[25]

Shortly after Hill wrote this, the Union Pacific, the Northern Pacific, and the Santa Fe all went bankrupt and had to be reorganized. This didn't surprise Hill; he gloated, "You will recall how often it has been said that when the Nor Pac, Union Pac and other competitors failed, our company would not be able to stand. . . . Now we have them all in bankruptcy. . .while we have gone along and met their competition." In fact, the efficient Hill cut his costs 13 percent from 1894 to 1895.

Hill criticized the grab for subsidies, but here is the ironic twist: those who got federal aid ended up being hung by the strings that were attached to it. In other words, there is some cause and effect between Hill's having no subsidy and prospering and the other transcontinentals' getting aid and going bankrupt. First, the subsidies, whether in loans or land, were always given on the basis of each mile completed. In this arrangement, as we have seen, the incentive was not to build a quality line, as Hill did, but to build quickly to get the aid. This resulted not only in poorly built lines but in poorly surveyed lines as well. Steep gradients meant increased fuel costs; poor building meant costly repairs and accidents along the line. Hill had no subsidy, so he built slowly and methodically. "During the past two years," Hill said in 1884, "we have spent a great deal of money for steel rails, ballasting track, transfer yards, terminal facilities, new equipment, new shops, and in fact we have put the road in better condition than any railway similarly situated that I know of. . . ." Hill, then, had lower fixed costs than did his subsidized competitors.[26]

By building the Great Northern without government interference, Hill enjoyed other advantages as well. He could build his line as he saw fit. Until Carnegie's triumph in the 1890s, American rails were inferior to some foreign rails, so Hill bought English and German rails for the Great Northern. The subsidized transcontinentals were required in their charters to buy American-made steel, so they were stuck with the lesser product. Their charters also required them to carry government mail at a discount, and this cut into their earnings. Finally, without Congressional approval, the subsidized railroads could not build spur lines off the main line. Hill's Great Northern, in contrast, looked like an octopus, and he credited spur lines as critical to his success.

In debating the Pacific Railway Bill in the 1860s, some Congressmen argued that even if the federally funded transcontinentals proved to be inefficient, they should still be aided because they would increase the social rate of return to the United States. Some historians and economists, led by Robert Fogel, have picked up this argument, and it goes like this: the UP made little profit and was poorly built, but it increased the value of the land along the road and promoted farms and cities in areas that could not have supported them without cheap transportation. Fogel claims that the value of land along a forty-mile strip on each side of the UP was worth $4.3 million in 1860 and $158.5 million by 1880. Without the UP, this land would have remained unsettled and the U. S. would not have had the national benefits of productive farms, new industries, and growing cities in the West. To the nation, then, the high social rate of return justified the building of the UP, CP, NP, and Santa Fe railroads.[27]

What this argument overlooks is the negative social, economic, and political return to the United States that came with using federal subsidies to build railroads. The first thing to recognize is that the gain in social return that Fogel describes is temporary. If the government had not subsidized a transcontinental, then private investors like Hill would have built them sooner and would have built them better. Subsidy promoters tried to deny this argument at the time, but Hill's achievement shows that it would have been done, only at a slower (but more efficient) pace. We can dismiss the widely promoted view expressed in Congress by Rep. James H. Campbell: "This [Union Pacific] road never could be constructed on terms applicable to ordinary roads. . . . It is to be constructed through almost impassable mountains, deep ravines, canyons, gorges, and over arid and sandy plains. The Government must come forward with a liberal hand, or the enterprise must be abandoned forever." The increase in social rate of return, then, would only be present until some private investor did what the government did first.[28]

Here is a key point: the gain in social return was only temporary, but the loss of shipping with an inefficient railroad was permanent. The UP and NP were, as we have seen, inefficient in gradients, curvature, length, quality of construction, repair costs, and use of fuel. This meant permanently high fixed costs for all passengers and freight using the subsidized transcontinentals.

The subsidizing of railroads cost the nation in other ways, too. First, the land that was given to the railroads could not be sold for revenue. Second, the giving of subsidies to one established a precedent and resulted in the giving of subsidies to many. When the government gave twenty million acres to the UP, the NP and others clamored for aid; the result was the giving of 131 million acres of land to various railroads. Third, the granting of all this land, and money too, made for shady business ethics and political corruption. The Credit Mobilier is an example of poor business ethics, and the CP's tight control over California politics is a sample of political corruption. Part of this corruption is reflected in the automatic monopolies that subsidized transcontinentals had. When Jay Gould doubled rates along parts of the UP, not much could be done. It took time to build privately financed lines; and, when they were done, they had to compete with a railroad that had, thanks to the government, millions of acres of free land and large cash reserves.

A final hidden cost of subsidizing railroads is seen in the mass of lawmaking, much of it harmful, all of it time-consuming, that state legislatures, Congress, and the Supreme Court did after watching the UP, CP, and NP in action. The publicizing of shoddy construction, the Credit Mobilier scandal, rate manipulating, and bankrupt health spas angered consumers; and angry consumers pestered their Congressmen to regulate the railroads. Much of the regulating, however, had unintended consequences and made the situation worse. For example, when the corruption in the building of the UP became known, there was public outrage followed by a congressional investigation. In the investigating, many were irritated that the UP had made no payment on its government loans. Congress, as we have seen, passed the Thurman Law, which forced the UP to pay 25 percent of its annual earnings toward retiring its $28 million debt to the government. The problem here is that the shoddy construction of the UP made for high fixed costs, and the lack of spur lines limited its chances for profits. This meant that the UP had to raise rates for passengers and freight to pay back its loans. The rate hikes, though, caused even more public outcry: many noticed, for example, that the UP and NP were charging more than the GN did; and this helped lead to demands for rate regulation. Congress obliged and, in 1887, created the Interstate Commerce Commission to investigate and abolish rate discrimination. This created two new problems: first, it was now illegal to give discounts. Hill argued that rate cutting had led to lower rates over the years and that this allowed the United States to capture a larger share of overseas trade. Hill insisted that the ICC law, if enforced (which it eventually was), would hurt railroads in domestic and overseas trade. Second, the ICC law eventually cost the taxpayers millions of dollars every year; it created a need for thousands of federally funded bureaucrats to listen to shippers all over the nation and to snoop into the detailed records of almost every railroad in the country.[29]

The issue of foreign trade is important and was hotly disputed during Congress' debates on the transcontinentals. Advocates of federal aid strongly argued that subsidized railroads would capture foreign trade and increase national wealth. "Commerce is power and empire," said Senator William M. Gwin of California. "Give us, as this [Union Pacific] Railroad would, the permanent control of the commerce and exchanges of the world, and in the progress of time and the advance of civilization, we would command the institutions of the world." Yet the UP and NP were so inefficient, they couldn't even capture or develop the trade of their own regions, least of all the world. If Hill hadn't come along and built the privately financed Great Northern, the United States might have forever lost opportunities to capture Oriental markets.[30]

Once he completed the GN, he studied the opportunities for trade in the Orient and marveled at its potential. "If the people of a single province of China should consume [instead of rice] an ounce a day of our flour," Hill wistfully said, "they would need 50,000,000 bushels of wheat per annum, or twice the Western surplus." The key, Hill believed, was "low freight rates"; and these he intended to supply. In 1900, he plowed six million dollars into his Great Northern Steamship Company and shuttled two steamships back and forth from Seattle to Yokohama and Hong Kong. Selling wheat was only one of Hill's ideas. He tried cotton, too. Ever the pump-primer, Hill told a group of Japanese industrialists he would send them cheap Southern cotton, and deliver it free, if they would use it along with the short-staple variety they got from India. If they didn't like it, they could have a refund and keep the cotton. This technique worked, and Hill filled many boxcars and steamships with Southern cotton destined for Japan. Hill's railroads and steamships also carried New England textiles to China. In 1896, American exports to Japan were only $7.7 million; but nine years later, with Hill in command, this figure jumped to $51.7 million.[31]

An even greater coup may have been Hill's capturing of the Japanese rail market. Around 1900, Japan began a railroad boom and England and Belgium made bids to supply the rails. In this case, the Japanese may have underestimated Hill: it didn't seem likely that he could be competitive if he had to buy rails in Pittsburgh, ship them to the Great Northern, carry them by rail to Seattle, then by steamship to Yokohama. Hill was so efficient, though, and so eager for trade in Asia, that he underbid the English and the Belgians by $1.50 per ton and captured the order for 15,000 tons of rails. Hill was spearheading American dominance in the Orient.[32]

Hill worked diligently to market the exports of the Northwest. Wheat from the plains, copper from Montana, and apples from Washington all got Hill's special attention. Without Hill's low freight rates and aggressive marketing, some of these Northwest products might never have been competitive to export. Washington and Oregon, for example, were covered with Western pine and Douglas fir trees. But it was Southern pine that had dominated much of the American lumber market. Hill could provide the lowest freight rates, but he needed someone to risk harvesting the Western lumber. He found Frederick Weyerhauser, his next-door neighbor, and sold him 900,000 acres of Western timberland at $6.00 an acre. Then Hill cut freight costs from ninety to forty cents per hundred pounds, and the two of them captured some of the Midwestern lumber market and prospered together.[33]

Hill became America's greatest railroad builder, he believed, because he followed a consistent philosophy of business. First, build the most efficient line possible. Second, use this efficient line to promote the exports in your section—in other words you must help others before you can be helped. Third, do not overextend; expand only as profits allow. Hill would probably have agreed with Thomas Edison that genius is one percent inspiration and 99 percent perspiration. Few people were willing to exert the perspiration necessary to learn the railroad business and apply these principles. Many, like Villard, Gould, and Stanford, took the easy route and chased subsidies, hiked rates, and manipulated stock; but this approach never built a winning railroad. "If the Northern Pacific could be handled as we handle our property," Hill said, "it could be made [a] great property . . . but it has not been run as a railway for years, but as a device for creating bonds to be sold." Hill understood markets, prices, and human nature; when he saw what his rivals were doing, he ceased to fear them.

The only thing that Hill did seem to fear was the potential for damage when the federal government stepped in to direct the economy. He understood why this happened—why people pressured Congress to involve itself in economic matters. California, isolated on the Pacific coast, wanted the cheap goods that a railroad would bring. So Senator Gwin lobbied in Congress for the UP. American steel producers wanted to sell more steel, so they pushed Congress to put a tariff on imported steel. Hill's problem was that, when his rivals were subsidized and when tariffs forced him to pay 50 percent more for English steel, he had to be twice as good to survive. One way out, which Hill took, was to support those politicians in the Northwest who would fight subsidies and high tariffs, and who would urge Congress to give him the right-of-way through Indian land.[34]

What Hill ultimately deplored more than tariffs and subsidies were the ICC and the Sherman Anti-trust Act. Congress passed these vague laws to protest rate hikes and monopolies. They were passed to satisfy public clamor (which was often directed at wrong-doing committed by Hill's subsidized rivals). Because they were vaguely written, they were harmless until Congress and the Supreme Court began to give them specific meaning. And here came the irony: laws that were passed to thwart monopolists, were applied to thwart Hill.

The ICC, for example, was created in 1887 to ban rate discrimination. The Hepburn Act, passed in 1906, made it illegal for railroads to charge different rates to different customers. This law was partly aimed at rate manipulators like Jay Gould. But it ended up striking Hill, who now could not offer rate discounts on exports traveling on the Great Northern en route to the Orient. Hill had given the Japanese and Chinese special rates on American cotton, wheat, and rails to wean them to American exports. But the Hepburn Act, according to Hill, immediately cut in half American trade to these countries. Hill testified vigorously during the Senate hearings that preceded the Hepburn Act, but was ignored. He was furious that he now had to publish his rates and give all shippers anywhere the special discount he was giving the Asians to capture their business. Since he couldn't do this and survive, he eventually sold his ships and almost completely abandoned the Asian trade.[35]

"Rates vary with conditions," Hill said.

> They vary from day to day, almost. I was much struck by some of the questions [addressed to the previous witness during the Hepburn Act hearings] as the difficulty in fixing what is a reasonable rate by law. You are dealing with the questions that exist today. Can you apply the conditions that exist today to tomorrow or next week or next month? It is absolutely impossible. . . .

The Hepburn Act, though, said rates had to be made public, applied equally to all shippers, and could not be changed without thirty days notice. American exports to Japan and China dropped 40 percent ($41 million) between 1905 and 1907, and we will never know how much trade, domestic and foreign, was lost elsewhere.[36]

Another federal law that was aimed at others, but which struck

Hill instead, was the Sherman Anti-trust Act. As written, the Sherman Act banned "every combination. . .in restraint of trade." This vaguely written law was an immediate problem because every act of trade potentially restrains other trade. This meant that the courts would have to decide what the law meant. The first test of the Sherman Act, the *E. C. Knight* case (1895), liberated entrepreneurs to freely buy and sell. The American Sugar Refining Company had bought the E. C. Knight company and thereby held 98 percent of the American sugar market. The Supreme Court upheld this acquisition because no one had tried to "put a restraint upon trade or commerce." No one stopped anyone else from producing sugar and competing with American Sugar Refining. Therefore, the trade was legal even though "the result of the transaction. . .was creation of a monopoly in the manufacture of a necessary of life. . . ." In fact, other sugar producers did enter the market and steadily whittled the market share of American Sugar Refining from 98 to 25 percent by 1927.[37]

With the *E. C. Knight* case the law of the land, Hill saw no problem when he created the Northern Securities Company in 1901. After the Panic of 1893, Hill bought a controlling interest in the bankrupt NP and sometimes used it to ship his own freight. In 1901, Hill added the Chicago, Burlington, and Quincy to his holdings; this allowed him to tap markets to the south in lumber, meat-packing, and cotton. That same year he placed his stock in the GN, NP, and CB&Q in a holding company called the Northern Securities Company. Hill pointed out that in doing this he was not restraining trade; he was combining three smaller companies he already controlled into one larger company. Actually, competition among the transcontinentals was keener than ever. Edward H. Harriman had taken over the bankrupt UP after the Panic of 1893 and, free of governmental restrictions, had plowed $25 million into new track, new routes, new equipment, and spur lines. He adopted Hill's philosophy of building an efficient railroad and promoting the exports of the region. Harriman even bought steamships and prepared to challenge Hill in the Orient. When Harriman tried to buy into the NP, a stock fight resulted, and financier J. P. Morgan suggested the creating of a holding company, the Northern Securities, to prevent stock manipulation on Wall Street. Hill would be president of the Northern Securities and therefore keep control of his three railroads; Harriman would serve on the board of directors. Competition was not stifled; in fact, rates fell on both the GN and the UP in the two years after the Northern Securities was created.[38]

Hill was therefore disappointed when President Theodore Roosevelt urged the Supreme Court to strike down the Northern Securities under the Sherman Act. He called the Northern Securities a "very arrogant corporation" and Hill a "trust magnate, who attempts to do what the law forbids." But, of course, no one knew what the Sherman Act did or did not forbid. To lead his defense, Hill hired John G. Johnson, who was the "successful warrior" in the *E. C. Knight* case. Johnson defended the Northern Securities in much the same way he had defended the E. C. Knight Company. He argued that the Northern Securities did not restrain trade or bar other railroads from entering the Northwest; he then attacked the Sherman Act for being "so obscurely written that one cannot tell when he is violating [it]. . . ." With the *E. C. Knight* case as a precedent, with rates falling on Hill's railroads, and with competition stiff between the GN and the UP, Johnson argued his case with confidence.[39]

In 1904, however, in a landmark case, the Supreme Court decided five to four against the Northern Securities. It had to be dissolved. Hill was especially irritated at Justice John M. Harlan, who wrote the majority opinion. The Northern Securities was, according to Harlan, "within the meaning of the [Sherman] Act, a 'trust'; but if it is not it is a combination in restraint of interstate and international commerce; and that is enough to bring it under the condemnation of the act." Harlan continued with a devastating statement: "The mere existence of such a combination. . .constitute[s] a menace to, and a restraint upon, that freedom of commerce which Congress intended to recognize and protect, and which the public is entitled to have protected."[40]

The *Northern Securities* decision, then, overturned the *E. C. Knight* case. Now "the mere existence" of a large corporation was seen as a threat to trade and therefore unlawful. Justice Oliver Wendell Holmes wrote a dissent which credited this astonishing verdict to an unsophisticated, but widespread belief among the public, in Congress, and in the courts that big corporations must necessarily be bad ones. "Great cases," Holmes concluded, "make bad law." Meanwhile Hill had to abolish the Northern Securities, as well as his trade with the Orient.[41]

The Bettmann Archive

James J. Hill: "Our own line [the Great Northern] was built without any government aid."

A look at the story of Hill and the railroads shows again the harmful, but unintended consequences that followed federal tinkering with the economy. The goals for federal intervention sounded so noble: subsidize a railroad to conquer the West and then the world; strike down those corporations that "restrain trade." Yet these noble goals were soon lost in an eddy of tragic consequences. In the case of the Sherman Act, Harlan's interpretation was applied again and again. Since "the mere existence of such a combination" as the Northern Securities was bad, all large corporations now had to fear prosecution. Just how much this hurt American trade, at home and abroad will never be known. Robert Sobel and other business historians have argued that this fear of being too big made some corporations stifle innovation and reduce their dominance in their industries in order to protect inefficient competitors. General Motors and IBM are frequently cited as examples of companies that dulled their competitive edge to help their rivals survive.[42]

Hill was sad and predicted that the ICC and the Sherman Act would ruin American railroads and threaten cheap trade throughout the nation. A 72-year-old Hill would even write a book, *Highways of Progress*, to argue this point. But his last days seem to have been happy. He had built the best railroad in America and had used it to beat subsidized rivals time and again. He helped open the Northwest to settlement and the Orient to American trade. He had made a difference in the way the world worked. To some viewers, he was the real hero in the drama of the American transcontinental railroads.

"Confidence and unity of purpose"

Courtesy, William W. Scranton

Joseph Scranton

Copy photography by Dorothy Allen from an original in the Lackawanna Historical Society Archives

George W. Scranton

Selden T. Scranton

CHAPTER THREE

The Scrantons and America's First Iron Rails

Steamships and transcontinental railroads were obviously important to America's industrial revolution. Even more critical, however, was the iron and steel industry itself. A successful iron industry could be the means of manufacturing a variety of cheap products to sell at home and abroad. With iron, for example, Americans could mass-produce rails and use them to cut transportation costs, open markets out west, and speed new products to cities throughout the nation. In the world of the 1800s, if a nation could produce cheap iron and steel, it could shape its own destiny.

The problem for America was that Englishmen controlled the world's iron markets. They had developed the first blast furnaces, and they had also invented the puddling techniques needed to purify molten iron. They likewise had a generation of skilled iron-makers eager to compete on a world market. In short, they had a large head start and, during the 1830s, used it to build all of America's iron rails. They also sent America iron-tipped plows, locks, nails, and all of the cast-iron pipes used for the nation's water system. By 1840, dozens of Americans were frantically tinkering with different types of fuels, ores, and blast furnaces, trying to produce American-made iron.[1]

In 1839, Nicholas Biddle, the former president of the Bank of the United States, lamented, "With all the materials for supplying iron in our own lands, the country has been obliged to pay enormous sums to Europeans for this necessary article. . . . This dependence is horrible." This "costly humiliation," Biddle urged, "ought to cease forever." Rails were especially needed; and, six years later, the *American Railroad Journal* complained: "The American iron-masters appear to consider railroad iron as unworthy of their notice. . . . Not a bar of T-rail has yet been rolled in the three great anthracite and iron districts of Pennsylvania."[2]

During the 1840s, Pennsylvania's Lackawanna Valley, in the northeast part of the state, would be the battleground where American independence from English iron would be fought and won. This masterpiece of entrepreneurship was largely the work of George, Selden, and Joseph Scranton, who, after much experimenting, became the first Americans to mass-produce rails.[3] In doing so they harnessed talent, capital, and technical expertise from within their families and friends, investors in small towns in the Lackawanna Valley, and outsiders from New York. Two things are striking: first, the Lackawanna Valley, with its thinly scattered, low-quality ore deposits, was hardly a natural setting for manufacturing; second, in the competition for urban growth, the winning city of Scranton did not exist until the 1840s. Nearby Wilkes-Barre and Carbondale had the advantages of age and wealth, until Scranton overcame them.[4]

The migration of the visionary Scrantons to northeast Pennsylvania began in 1839, when William Henry, a trained geologist, scoured the area looking for the right ingredients for iron-making—water power, anthracite coal, iron ore, lime, and sulphur. He found these elements near Wilkes-Barre, the oldest, largest, and wealthiest city in northeast Pennsylvania. Wilkes-Barre's leaders, though, were cautious: they preferred to ship coal safely down the Susquehanna River, not to risk their fortunes on unproven iron. They rejected Henry's "attempts to raise a company in the Wyoming Valley [Wilkes-Barre] for an iron concern." So Henry went about twenty miles east into the wilderness of the Lackawanna Valley, and looked over the land in this area. It had some water power and, of course, lots of anthracite; he also found small quantities of iron ore and lime, so he falsely assumed they existed there in abundance.[5]

Playing a hunch, Henry took an option to buy 500 acres of land at present-day Scranton and built a blast furnace on it. At first he sought the necessary $20,000 for the scheme from New York and England; but the high risk of his daring experiment frightened away even the hardiest of speculators. Finding greater faith from his family, Henry received support from his son-in-law, Selden Scranton, and Scranton's brother George, both of whom were operating the nearby Oxford Iron Works in Oxford, New Jersey. Originally from Connecticut, the wide-ranging Scrantons tapped their credit lines and picked up additional capital from their first cousin, Joseph Scranton;

his brother-in-law, Joseph C. Platt; and friends, Sanford Grant, and John and James Blair, who were merchants and bankers in Belvidere, New Jersey. These entrepreneurs, which we will call the Scranton group, raised $20,000 in 1840 and spent the next two years building the blast furnace and digging the ore and coal to make iron.[6]

Making iron, they quickly discovered, required more entrepreneurship than they had originally expected. The local ores and limestone were limited and of poor quality. They had chosen the wrong location, but it was too late to sell out and switch so they searched eastern Pennsylvania and New Jersey for the right combination of ores and limestone. As the *Iron Manufacturers's Guide* later understated: "The absence of anthracite iron deposits becomes a subject of curious speculation as it has been one of great pecuniary interest and was a bitter disappointment to the first manufacturers of iron with stone [anthracite] coal."[7]

Only the local coal lived up to expectations, and this was available in other areas with established cities closer to the lime and ore. When the Scrantons made their iron, they brought their lime and ore on boats from Danville, Pennsylvania, about thirty miles up the Susquehanna River right by the mansions on the River Common in Wilkes-Barre and over land almost twenty miles to Scranton.[8]

The high costs of transportation and the unexpected purchases of ore and lime almost ran the Scrantons into bankruptcy; then George Scranton came up with a plan to convert the pig-iron into nails. Such a bold venture into manufacturing would not be cheap. The need for a rolling mill and a nail factory upped the ante to $86,000. Desperate for credit, George Scranton coaxed some of this money from New Yorkers. Yet this jeopardized the family's ownership. So he placed his greatest reliance on other members of the Scranton group: long-time friends John and James Blair invested money from their bank in New Jersey, and Joseph Scranton sent funds from his mercantile business in Augusta, Georgia. By 1843, George Scranton got his $86,000, kept control within the family, and began making nails for markets throughout the east coast.[9]

The nail factory failed miserably. First, no rivers or rails helped market its product. Dependent on land transportation, the Scrantons transferred the nails on wagons east to Carbondale and west to the Susquehanna River and from there shipped them to other markets. Second, no one wanted the Scrantons' nails because they were poor in quality. The low-grade ores in the Lackawanna Valley provided only brittle and easily breakable nails. Faced with bankruptcy, the Scrantons contemplated the conversion of the nail mill into a rolling mill for railroad tracks. Experienced Englishmen still dominated the world production of rails in the 1840s; no American firm had dared to challenge them. After floundering in the production of nails, however, the Scrantons decided that a lucrative rail contract might be the gamble that could restore their lost investment.[10]

As luck would have it, in 1846, the nearby New York and Erie Railroad had a contract with the state of New York to build a rail line 130 miles from Port Jervis to Binghamton, New York. When Englishmen hesitated to supply the Erie with the needed rails, the Scrantons had their chance. They traveled to New York and boldly persuaded the board of directors of the New York and Erie to give their newly formed company the two-year contract for producing 12,000 tons of T-rails. They promised to supply rails cheaper and quicker than the British. Impressed with the Scrantons and desperate for rails, the directors of the New York and Erie advanced $90,000 to the eager Scrantons to construct a rolling mill and to furnish the necessary track.[11]

The construction of the mill and the making of thousands of tons of rails seemed impossible. The contract called for the Scrantons to supply the Erie with rails in less than twenty months. The Scrantons would first have to learn how to make the rails they promised to provide. Building the blast furnaces would come next. Then they would have to import some ore and much limestone into the Lackawanna Valley to make the rails. Finally, because they lacked a water route to the Erie line, they would have to draft dozens of teams of horses to carry finished rails from their rolling mills scores of miles through the wilderness and up mountains to New York, right where the track was laid. It is no wonder the New Yorkers wanted to back out at the last moment. Yet somehow, in less than a year and a half, the Scrantons did it. On December 27, 1848, just four days before the expiration of the Erie's charter, the Scrantons fulfilled their contract and completed the rail line.[12]

An interesting feature of the Scrantons' achievement was that they built their rails during a time of low tariffs. Some businessmen have always argued that their government should place high tariffs on imports to protect local manufacturers against foreign competitors. Yet, in 1846, the year the Scrantons began making rails, Congress passed the Walker Tariff, which lowered duties on imported rails and other iron products from England. George Scranton actually said he liked the lower tariff for two reasons. First, the Scranton price of $65 per ton of rail was already fixed and was competitive with English prices. In any case, Scranton estimated his firm would be earning $20 per ton profit, so the tariff was not needed. Second, the low tariff meant that the Scrantons could buy their raw materials—pig iron, rolled bars, and hammered bars—more cheaply. This would, Scranton hoped, lay the foundation for his firm to be the strongest on the continent for years to come.[13]

Many Americans were amazed that an iron works located in the middle of a wilderness, with no connecting links to outside markets, could build and deliver 130 miles of rails to a railroad in another state. The Scrantons did not want to have to duplicate this feat, so they did two things to improve their location: first, they started building a city around their iron works; second, they began building a railroad to connect their city to outside markets. That way they could ship rails anywhere in the country and also export the local anthracite, which could be sold as a home-heating fuel.[14]

With the confidence of New York investors, the Scrantons proposed two railroads: the Liggett's Gap, and the Delaware and Cobb's Gap. The Liggett's Gap line, running from Scranton fifty-six miles north to connect with the Erie at Great Bend, would permit Scranton to supply coal to the farms in the Genessee Valley in upstate New York; the Delaware and Cobb's Gap route, running sixty-four miles east to the Delaware River at Stroudsburg, would give the Scrantons a potential outlet for coal to New York City. By backing two lines, the Scrantons gave themselves two markets for Lackawanna Valley coal. The building of a railroad, then, was a logical sequel to the Scrantons' superb iron works. The railroad itself became a market for Scranton iron, it provided an outlet for Scranton coal, and it promoted trade for Scranton city.[15]

Building these two railroads was no cinch. Some of the terrain was mountainous: even after using gunpowder to level the hills, the grade was still steep (eight feet to the mile) in places. Also, George Scranton had to negotiate some delicate right-of-way problems with farmers along the rail route who were overvaluing their land. Of course, the Scrantons were using their own homemade rails for the line, but this still ran into costs. For all of this, the Scrantons needed more New York capital, but they had to be careful. They wanted to be entrepreneurs, not pawns of the New Yorkers. The Scrantons had to make sure they retained a guiding interest in their projects. This they did. The two railroads were surveyed and built from 1850 to 1853; they both were consolidated into one line, the Delaware, Lackawanna, and Western Railroad (hereafter Lackawanna Railroad) with George Scranton as its first president. In 1853, flushed with success, the Scrantons also incorporated their iron works as the Lackawanna Iron and Coal Company (hereafter Lackawanna Company) with $800,000 in stock; they elected Selden Scranton as president.[16]

The building of America's premier iron works and railroad was an amazing feat of collective entrepreneurship. The Scranton group became unified behind a vision of mass-produced rails, the creating of a city, and the laying of rails from its borders east and north to outside markets. As individuals, the members of the Scranton group had few of the skills and little of the capital needed to fulfill this vision; but collectively they did. They had to have outside cash, but their confidence and unity of purpose impressed New York investors and convinced them the Scrantons could do the job.[17]

Not everyone wished the Scrantons well. And this made their success story even more remarkable. First, there was the generally negative reaction from leaders in Wilkes-Barre, who thought the rise of a new city would threaten their hegemony in northeast Pennsylvania. The Scrantons logically tried to secure loans in Wilkes-Barre, the oldest and largest city in the area. But the businessmen there rarely helped, and they often hurt. For example, in the 1850s the Scrantons tried to get a charter for their railroad from the state legislature; Wilkes-Barre's able and influential politicians thwarted the Scrantons because the new rail line threatened Wilkes-Barre's trade dominance along the Susquehanna River through the North Branch Canal. Referring to Wilkes-Barre as "the old harlot of iniquity," a concerned lawyer advised the Scrantons that those associated with the North Branch Canal in Wilkes-Barre "all make common cause against [the] Liggett's Gap [Railroad]."[18]

Not only did politicians in Wilkes-Barre hamper iron production and delay rail completion, they prevented the Scrantons' emerging industrial city from becoming a county seat. The new city of Scranton happened to be situated in the eastern end of Luzerne County. So wily politicians in the county seat of Wilkes-Barre used statewide influence to delay for decades the creation of a new county. Even the prestige and influence of George Scranton in the Pennsylvania Senate and U. S. Congress during the 1850s could not force the division of Luzerne County. So while the Scrantons were trying to promote their new town as a Mecca of industrial opportunity, the town's administrative business was being diverted to the county seat of Wilkes-Barre. Summarizing Wilkes-Barre's general "policy of obstruction," Benjamin Throop observed that

> during all these early struggles, Wilkes-Barre had the advantage. The Lackawanna Valley was poor, and had its fortune still to make; Wilkes-Barre had inherited considerable wealth from its former generations. The public-spirited men here were, most of them, new-comers and unknown. Those of the opposition had prestige and influence.[19]

Possibly even more damaging than the opposition from Wilkes-Barre's politicians was the hostility from many local farmers near Scranton. These old settlers liked the prospects of improved transportation to get their crops to market, but many did not want to see the "machine" transform their "garden" into an industrial community.[20] One local observer described their fears sarcastically as follows:

> There were then, as there are yet, and as there always will be, a debilitated, but croaking class of persons who by some hidden process manage to keep up a little animation in their useless bodies, who gathered in bar-room corners, and who, with peculiar wisdom belonging to this class while discussing weighty matters, gravely predicted that "the Scrantons must fail!"[21]

Even before the Scrantons arrived, several of these farmers had formed a committee and denounced "blackleg drivellers, in the shape of incorporated companies."[22]

The local squabbles with the old settlers regularly kept the Scrantons from fully attending to their iron works. Recognizing this problem early, the Scrantons donated land and labor to help build the old settlers a church. Through a company store, the industrialists enthusiastically traded goods and produce with nearby farmers. Desperate for credit, though, the Scrantons were barely surviving in the early 1840s and had to seek extensions on local loans. At one point William Henry wrote, "We have not twenty-five cents in hand. . . . The credit of the concern [is] impaired." He added, "This suspense and uncertainty is worse where our credit is concerned than almost any other mode of proceeding." George Scranton felt the same way. At one point he described himself as being "worried most to death for fear we can't meet all [credit obligations]. . . . I cannot stand trouble & excitement as I could once. I don't sleep good. My appetite is poor & digestion bad. . . . If we can succeed in placing [the] Lacka[wanna iron works] out of debt it would help me much. . . ." During some of the Scrantons' darker moments, "every petty claim of indebtedness was urged and pressed before the justices of the township with an earnestness really annoying."[23]

Disputes with the old settlers over land and credit, then, persisted as the Scrantons verged for years on bankruptcy without successfully producing nails or rails. At one extreme, a vindictive local merchant threatened to "break. . .down" the Scrantons' company store by "selling goods very cheap"—if necessary by "giving away his goods." At the other end, legend has it that after the Scrantons' brittle nails were rejected by New York merchants, Selden Scranton immediately sold quantities of the "practically worthless" product to unsuspecting old settlers. Such feuding seems to have been commonplace; even when the Scrantons finally received the rail contract from the Erie, many farmers withheld the use of their mules and horses to prevent delivery of the rails; others charged exorbitant prices.[24] Under these conditions, one can hardly argue that the location of Scranton was inevitably destined for urban glory. It was not.

When the iron works and the railroad succeeded, the Scrantons then promoted the growth of their new city. Their correspondence shows that they clearly viewed industrial and urban growth as symbiotic. Their investment in real estate and housing multiplied in value after the success of their iron works and the arrival of a railroad. The Scranton group originally bought a 500-acre tract for $8,000 in 1840. As mere coal land that acreage was worth at least $400,000 by the mid-1850s. As improved land much of it was worth even more. The Scrantons had laid out streets, sold lots, and built mansions for themselves and company houses for their workers.[25]

Unlike the leaders in Wilkes-Barre and Carbondale, the Scranton group created an open environment for their city and actively recruited investors to come. To do this effectively, they went to the state legislature in 1866 and secured wide city limits of almost twenty square miles, which at that time included mostly farm and timberland. They incorporated this large space to fulfill their vision of their city's future, in which they saw many more industries, homes, and parks. The space was needed to plan all this properly.[26]

Wilkes-Barre's leaders, by contrast, wanted to limit immigration and preserve their closed society. They intentionally settled for small

Copy photography by Dorothy Allen from an orginal in the Lackawanna Historical Society Archives

Scranton, 1840. "The Scrantons believed their city would grow, and they diligently planned its expansion."

Copy photography by Dorothy Allen from an orginal in the Lackawanna Historical Society Archives

Scranton, 1883

city limits of 4.14 square miles and did not even incorporate this much land until five years after the Scrantons did so. This made urban planning in Wilkes-Barre difficult, and it also hindered the preventing of fires and the controlling of epidemics.[27]

Carbondale became an even more dreadful example of urban planning. Most industrial cities in the nineteenth century were hardly paragons of cleanliness and safety, but Carbondale was among the dingiest. Fires periodically gutted whole sections of the city, destroying property, buildings, and lives. Mines caved in from time to time; the most serious collapse buried sixty miners (fourteen died) in forty acres of subterranean caverns. Floods were also a threat. One flood, caused by a poorly planned reservoir, surged through the main street, filling the mines, taking lives, and annihilating buildings and houses.

In light of these disorderly influences, it is startling to discover that, before 1851, Carbondale had no fire or police department. In that year, after an unusually severe fire "laid waste to the greater portion of the city above the public square," Carbondale's shortsighted leaders finally decided to get some "means of protection against fire or outlaws." The dedication of Carbondale's new civil servants seems to have been slim because another fire soon ravaged the city, this time "entailing a considerable loss" to William Richmond's coal-car factory and George L. Dickson's mercantile firm, among other damage. This new city government apparently made no provision for sanitation; as one resident complained in 1875, "Another inconvenience is that citizens have no convenient place to dump their coal ashes, or empty. . .rubbish." Such a perilous environment prevented a stable business climate and may have helped push Richmond, Dickson, and other entrepreneurs out of Carbondale and into Scranton.[28]

All of this creates the impression that, once the iron works and the railroad were established, and once the city of Scranton was incorporated, the Scranton group had it made. But this was not the case; in fact, most of the Scranton group did not die rich, and two died very poor. William Henry, the original leader of the group, left the city in the 1840s after some bad investments. Henry had energy and vision but little patience and endurance; he died embittered and impoverished in 1878. Sanford Grant, the first owner of the company store, wilted when faced with business competition and industrial risk. Selling his stock, he left for safer business climes in Belvidere, New Jersey, where he lived, without ulcers or wealth, until his death in the 1880s. Displaying greater fortitude than Grant, Selden Scranton became the first president of the Lackawanna Company; five years later, though, he and his brother Charles left to operate a blast furnace in Oxford, New Jersey. Their iron-making talents ultimately failed them; Selden declared bankruptcy in 1884 and died shortly thereafter. George Scranton, the early leader and driving force behind coal and railroad development, had more faith and perseverance than most of the others. He amassed $200,000, built a fine mansion, and served as U.S. Congressman from northeast Pennsylvania. George, however, still lost some of his fortune during the Panic of 1857 and had to sell much of his stock in the Lackawanna Railroad at reduced value. Plagued with health problems from overwork during the rugged days of the 1840s, George died in 1861 at age forty-nine.[29]

Three other members of the Scranton group never abandoned their vision of manufacturing rails and building a city; they achieved fabulous success and wealth. On top was Joseph Scranton, who said at the start, "I have no fears of the ultimate success [of the iron works],. . .I have invested in it. Should remain till it is doubled or lost as the case may be." Twenty-seven years later, Scranton was president of the flourishing Lackawanna Iron and Coal Company and was worth $1,100,000, making him the wealthiest man in northeast Pennsylvania. His brother-in-law and next-door neighbor, Joseph C. Platt, was superintendent of the Lackawanna Company and was worth $220,000. Right behind Joseph Scranton with $910,000 was his friend James Blair, who had backed the Scrantons from nails to rails. Blair held lots of stock in both the iron works and the railroad; he then expanded and started Scranton's first trolley company.[30]

Some people point to such wealth, and the absence of it in other households, and argue that the state should redistribute it, or at least tax it at high rates. It hardly seems fair, they might say, that some people should have so little, while three men—Joseph Scranton, Joseph Platt, and James Blair—should own close to ten percent of all the wealth in the city (according to the data in the 1870 federal manuscript census). As socialist Harold Laski once said, "Less government. . .means liberty only for those who control the sources of economic power." What we need, according to this view, is an active state to transfer income, chop up inheritances, perhaps even to impose equality of condition.

To argue this way is to miss a key point: Scranton's founders, as entrepreneurs, created something out of nothing. They created their assets and created opportunities for others when they successfully bore the risks of making America's first iron rails. Without them, almost everybody else in the region would have been poorer. The amount of wealth in a region (or a country) is not fixed; in 1870, Scranton, Platt, and Blair got the biggest piece of the economic pie, but it was the biggest piece of a much larger pie—made so by what they cooked up when they came to Pennsylvania thirty years earlier.

When the Scrantons came to the Lackawanna Valley, it was a poor farming region with no close ties to outside markets. In 1850, according to the federal manuscript census, no one in the Lackawanna Valley was worth more than $10,000. In 1870, after the Scrantons had established their city and their iron works, thirty-three families in Scranton alone were worth at least $100,000; and one was already a millionaire. Thousands of other families were working their way toward better lives. The Scrantons' iron works and railroad were the means to this end.[31]

Some people look at the results of splendid entrepreneurship and say that someone else might have come along later and done the same thing. We can see how improbable this is in the Scranton case. The wealthy leaders in the older, more prosperous city of Wilkes-Barre, for example, shunned manufacturing for years and often tried to thwart the Scranton's plans. If the Scrantons had not come along, much of the iron ore in central Pennsylvania and New Jersey would probably have been exported to Philadelphia, Pittsburgh, or New York, where more abundant capital would have eventually taken the risks of making manufactured goods. Northeast Pennsylvania would have been left in the dark.[32]

To be sure, the anthracite in the Lackawanna Valley was already attracting New York investors: but they came only to get coal, not to build cities and make the region prosper. Without dedicated local entrepreneurs, the Lackawanna Valley, like so many mining regions, would have enjoyed only fleeting and limited prosperity. The entrepreneurs in New York would have bought the coal land cheap, *then* supplied transportation to the region, collected their profits, and left the exporting area full of deserted mines and ghost towns.[33]

Let's look at the different opportunities the Scrantons, as entrepreneurs, created intentionally and unintentionally for others. First, the people in northeast Pennsylvania, especially those with capital to invest, now had new and better opportunities available. Scranton, in fact, became a magnet for entrepreneurs in nearby towns, except for Wilkes-Barre. Investors in the nearby county seats of Montrose and Towanda came to Scranton and set up the city's first two banks. From nearby Honesdale came Scranton's first large-scale flour miller. From Carbondale came the presidents of both of that city's banks, a locomotive builder, a stove maker, a coal operator, and the mayor. Not all of these men won fortunes, but several did, and their investments helped diversify Scranton's economy and made it one of the fastest growing cities in America in the late 1800s.[34]

Another group of winners were the many local farmers who held on to their land and sold it later as coal land. All they had to do was watch others do the work of establishing the region's export. After this, they cashed in. The Scrantons bore the risks of making rails from imported ore; then they risked building a railroad to connect the Lackawanna Valley to New York City. All the farmers had to do was hold on to their land and watch it rise in value—from $15 an acre in 1840 to $800 an acre in 1857. In just seventeen years, then, a 160-acre farm increased in worth from $2,400 to $128,000. Some of these locals even ended up richer than the wealthiest of the Scrantons. Benjamin Throop, for example, was a local physician who watched the Scrantons build their iron works; then he bought up much of the land in the area on the chance that they would succeed. He later wrote a book describing his real estate exploits and expressing his gratitude to the Scrantons. He even named his only son after George Scranton. When Throop died in 1897, at age 86, he left an estate of $10,000,000.[35]

Even immigrants could sometimes get rich in Scranton. The growth of Scranton from farming hamlet in 1840 to 45,000 people in 1880 brought thousands of immigrants to town. Many of them worked in the factories and improved their lives; they saved a little money and bought their own homes. Some of them had the talent and vision to rise to the top. In 1880, of Scranton's forty most prominent businessmen, measured by memberships on boards of directors, nine of them were immigrants. Some of these rags to riches immigrants were clearly among the most successful men in Scranton. Thomas Dickson, for example, came to America from Scotland and began work as a mule driver. Soon he was making engines, boilers, and locomotives for the Scrantons; he ended up as president of the Delaware and Hudson Railroad, a 500-mile line that linked Scranton to markets all over the east. Another immigrant, John Jermyn, came to Scranton in 1847 from England and began working for the Scrantons for 75 cents a day. Soon he was managing coal mines and was putting what little money he earned into coal land and real estate with a knack that amazed everyone. The critical risk in his career came in 1862, when he leased some abandoned mines northeast of Scranton. Defying the skeptics, Jermyn bought new machines and fulfilled a contract for one million tons of coal. He then tripled his contract and was on his way to becoming the largest independent coal operator in the Lackawanna Valley. A local credit agent said that Jermyn was "believed to be unaffected by the times, holding his own versus all contingencies." When he died in 1902, Jermyn left an estate of $7,000,000.[36]

Because the Scrantons did what they did, thousands of Americans had new opportunities in life. If they could just capture the Scrantons' vision, they had a chance to succeed. One life that was made anew was that of Joseph J. Albright, the uncle of Selden Scranton. Albright was in business near Nazareth, Pennsylvania, and went bankrupt in 1850, when he was nearly forty years old. He had to sell all his furniture at a sheriff's sale and deal with creditors from two states. He wrote Selden that "it is hard at my age to be thrown upon the world pennyless [sic]," and hoped that Selden's wife "wouldn't be ashamed of her poor friend." He even seems to have contemplated suicide and wrote that "death would have been a relief" to him.[37]

The Scranton group came to Albright's rescue and gave him a job as coal agent for their railroad. Soon Albright caught the Scrantons' vision. He was patient and invested wisely: he bought stock in the Scrantons' iron and coal company; he then joined them in building the city's gas and water system. On his own, he invested in a company to mill flour and in a firm to make locomotives. By 1872, he was worth half a million dollars and was elected president of the largest bank in the city. He had become a believer in Scranton and wanted to help the city that had given him a chance; when he died, he deeded his home to the city and gave $125,000 to build a major public library to help educate future generations in Scranton.[38]

Not everyone joined the Scranton team. Albright did, but another relative, Phillip Walter, also of Nazareth, resisted an elaborate courtship from the Scrantons in 1852. He told them he was reluctant "to pull [up] stakes and move" from "my long cherished home" because "I might fail." After a visit to Scranton, in which Walter sold hundreds of dollars worth of merchandise to an expanding population, he confessed that "I was quite enchanted with your place and the great, though undeserved, esteem in which I was held by many of the inhabitants." Walter also admitted, "I certainly could not find a place anywhere where I would rather go than to Scranton." He further acknowledged, "My sons. . .would likely find openings for business in such a thriving place as Scranton appears to be and will yet become." Other men of means saw these advantages and settled in Scranton. But Walter avoided getting "carried away by the admiration of your thriving place" by his reluctance to uproot and his haunting fear that "still I might fail." Winnowing out the conservative and the weak at heart, Scranton seems to have attracted a select set of venturesome leaders to guide its industrial growth.[39]

In building their city, the Scrantons consciously promoted entrepreneurship. The securing of wide city limits was part of this effort. They believed their city would grow, and they diligently planned its expansion. Along these lines, the Scrantons and their allies established a board of trade in 1867 to promote the industrial development of their city. They installed an innovative Welsh immigrant as the board's first president. The board actively recruited industry and even secured a law granting all new corporations tax-free status for their first ten years in Scranton.[40]

In this open environment, Scranton grew as a manufacturing center and attracted many capitalists who were willing to take different types of risks. This made for a combination of inventiveness and creative entrepreneurship. For example, Henry Boies came to Scranton from New York in 1865 and founded the successful Moosic Powder Company; then he perfected a gunpowder cartridge that reduced the death and injury resulting from carelessness in mining explosions. Boies seemed to court risky ventures and had failed twice before coming to Scranton. Once he had made his fortune in powder, the credit lines were open, and he went to work inventing a flexible steel wheel for locomotives. He started the Boies Steel Wheel Company in 1888 to manufacture his patented invention.[41]

Another innovation that succeeded in Scranton was Charles S. Woolworth's five-and-ten-cent store. Born in upstate New York, Woolworth, his brother Frank, and partner, Fred M. Kirby, experimented in the late 1870s with the opening of specialty stores featuring largely five-and-ten-cent merchandise. Shoppers were often skeptical of the first stores opened in Harrisburg, Lancaster, and York, Pennsylvania. In 1880, however, when Charles Woolworth set up a five-and-ten-cent store in Scranton, the idea caught on. The sales in Scranton were a modest $9,000 the first year, but the Woolworths and Kirby had laid the foundation for an empire, and Charles had found himself a new home in Scranton. A decade of brisk sales in Scranton encouraged Woolworth to start branch stores in New York and Maine in the 1890s. Kirby, meanwhile, started a profitable store in Wilkes-Barre. Soon Woolworths was selling nationally, and became a major American corporation. In Scranton, Woolworth joined with other local entrepreneurs in founding the International Textbook Company, which employed thousands of people to sell textbooks throughout the nation.[42]

The introduction of electricity in the 1880s brought out the best in Scranton's entrepreneurs. They didn't produce Thomas Edison; but they did have Merle J. Wightman, who designed and built one of the first motors to run trolley cars by electricity. Scranton also became one of the first cities in the nation to have an electric trolley system. Sensing opportunity, Wightman started his own company in Scranton to manufacture trolley engines on a large scale. Other Scrantonians tried to adapt electricity to coal mining. In 1894, they founded the Scranton Electric Construction Company, which perfected and manufactured electrical apparatus (e. g., mechanical drills, locomotive hoists, and mining pumps) for use throughout the anthracite coal fields.[43]

Scranton did not emerge inevitably as a center for manufacturing trolley motors, locomotive wheels, or textbooks. Nor was there any particular reason why Scranton should have become a major headquarters for directing a chain of five-and-ten-cent stores. Other cities throughout America had good enough location and transportation to have been sites for these industries. Even the making and distributing of electrical mining equipment could have been done in Wilkes-Barre or in anthracite towns other than Scranton. A key to Scranton's success seems to have been the presence of aggressive entrepreneurs, who had a philosophy of openness and commitment to growth. As the spiral of growth in industries, services, and population persisted, the city of Scranton, which was founded on a hunch, officially became one of the forty largest cities in the country in 1900.[44]

A lot can be learned from the story of the Scrantons. The first lesson is that entrepreneurs are needed to create wealth; when they succeed, others then have the chance to build on what they started. If we look at the later history of Scranton, we can also learn a second lesson: that it is hard for those on top to stay there in the generations that follow. An inheritance can be transferred; but entrepreneurship, talent, and vision cannot be. The industrial city of Scranton saw lots of movement down the ladder of social mobility, as well as up.

This can be seen if we look at what happened to the Scranton economic elite of 1880—those men who made up the first generation of the city's industrial leadership. I collected data on the forty men in Scranton who, by 1880, held the largest number of corporate directorships and major partnerships. These forty men dominated all of Scranton's major industries. Several were millionaires; and all had access to credit and contracts, which seemingly should have insured the success of their children in Scranton, which spiralled in population from 45,000 in 1880 to 137,000 in 1920.[45]

As founders and developers of the Scrantons' vision, these forty entrepreneurs had much to give their children. Blessed by the luck of the draw, these fortunate offspring could choose almost any career, with the security that only wealth can bring. Raised in Victorian mansions rife with servants, they often had doting parents to give them private-school education, college if they wanted, or specialized training in engineering or industry. If these children did not prosper, they could fall back on hefty inheritances. Also, as they matured, they could take advantage of Scranton's thriving marketplace to make even more money. By 1920, the sons of Scranton's 1880 leaders had ample opportunity to succeed their fathers as the pacesetters of Scranton's business world.[46]

Yet they did not. Few went hungry, but most could not come close to matching their father's achievements. Only nine of the forty economic leaders in 1880 had even one son, son-in-law, or grandson who forty years later was an officer of even one corporation in Scranton. In short, the fathers and sons provide a stunning contrast.[47]

The fathers built the city of Scranton, but why the sons did so poorly is complicated. Part of the reason for this startling breakdown lies in the general problem of family continuity. Six families didn't have any sons; seven others had too many—which splintered the family wealth into small pieces. In a very few cases, some sons left Scranton for business ventures elsewhere. Often the sons chose not to go into business: they led lives of brief and precarious leisure.

The fragmentation of some of Scranton's larger family fortunes seems remarkable. For example, brothers Thomas and George Dickson became president of a national railroad, the largest manufacturing company in northeast Pennsylvania, an iron company in New York, the vice president of the largest bank in Scranton, and directors on many large companies. Yet only one of Thomas Dickson's three sons went into business; and, under his leadership, the Dickson Manufacturing Company went out of business. George Dickson's only child, Walter, became a mere salesman and held no corporate influence. The four sons of multimillionaire James Blair were nonentities. Only one of Blair's sons appears to have been gainfully employed, and his job was that of assistant cashier in his father's bank.[48]

Even the Scrantons of Scranton were almost extinguished. George, Selden, and Joseph Scranton were the founding fathers of American rail making, but only one of their sons showed entrepreneurial skill. Selden was childless, and went bankrupt in any case. George was worth $200,000 when he died; but his sons, James and Arthur, became men of leisure, not entrepreneurs. Joseph's son William gave business a try, but his story was often sad. Joseph was president of the Lackawanna Iron and Coal Company from 1858 until his death in 1872. But during these years, the New Yorkers bought up so much stock that William was not allowed to succeed his father as company president. Young William was restless as a mere local manager, so he studied the new Bessemer process in Europe and returned to start his own Scranton Steel Company in 1881. The city's low tax on new industries gave him an edge over the larger Lackawanna Company, but the older company won the competition and absorbed his enterprise in 1891. William did prove to be a very capable builder and operator of the Scranton Gas and Water Company. He and his son, Worthington, ran this company profitably and, in 1928, Worthington sold it for $25 million.[49]

Some of the sons of Scranton's early industrialists literally squandered fortunes. Benjamin Throop, who was described earlier, became a millionaire in coal land and urban real estate. His surviving son had, at best, modest business skills, and when he and his wife died prematurely in 1894, the eighty-three-year-old Throop undertook the task of rearing his only grandchild, five-year-old Benjamin, Jr. The elder Throop died shortly thereafter, but young "Benny" inherited a ten-million-dollar fortune. Young Throop married into a prominent local family and, having no financial worries, began raising German shepherd dogs. He served in World War I, but by that time his wife had divorced him and he seems to have lost any interest that he might have had in gainful employment or in the city of Scranton. During the 1920s, like a character from an F. Scott Fitzgerald novel, he spent most of his time in Paris indulging champagne tastes in cars and women. He married a French movie star and traveled widely during their marriage. Throop died in 1935, in his mid-forties, of undisclosed stomach ailments after apparently dissipating his grandfather's entire fortune.[50]

Throop was a rare but not unique example of dissolution. Given the tradition of partible inheritance, many of the sons of economic leaders knew that they would never have to work, and so they became men of leisure with no business interests. For example, James Blair's son Austin was "a gentleman of leisure [with] [n]o[thing] to do except fish and hunt." According to a credit agent, "his fa[ther], James Blair, is a millionaire and supports him [and] lets him have a fine residence rent free and supplies him with funds when required."[51]

Without strong parental guidance, a slothful life was understandably attractive to these scions of wealth. Owing to the genetic improbability that Scranton's 1880 elite would produce only children like themselves, with a knack for business, the fragmenting of economic leadership should not surprise us. Edmund B. Jermyn's taste for horse racing—this son of the multimillionaire coal operator apparently "never missed a day's [horse] racing at Honesdale or at Goshen, N. Y."—becomes understandable. The son grew up under different conditions with different options in life from those that were available to his rags-to-riches father.[52]

The Throop and Blair families may provide clues to one possible relationship between parental guidance and entrepreneurship. On one hand, all of Benny Throop's parents and grandparents died before he was eight years old, so he had no family pressure to become a businessman and pass on the family fortune. The four sons of James Blair, on the other hand, had a long-lived father, who personally directed many of his own enterprises until his death at age ninety. The elder Blair outlived two of his sons, and the other two had passed middle age by the time they were independent of paternal control. By living so long and holding on so tightly to his investments, Blair may have quenched the spirit of entrepreneurship in his sons.

The role of the parents, the lack of business talent, the quest for leisure, and the problems of family continuity in general all seem to have combined to fragment the Scranton economic elite of 1880.

Of course, not all of Scranton's early industrialists had downwardly mobile sons. Nine of the forty top capitalists in the Scranton of 1880 passed the torch of leadership from father to son in 1920. In any randomly selected group of forty families, of course, some would produce sons or have sons-in-law with a flair for business. It is improbable, however, that nine of forty randomly chosen families would have corporate officers as sons. This merely shows that industrial leaders are much more likely than other groups in the population to father corporate officers. It does not show continuity of economic leadership because more than three-fourths of the industrial families of 1880 in Scranton failed to continue a line of corporate succession in the following generation.[53]

While most of the sons of entrepreneurs stumbled, a variety of new immigrants in Scranton saw their opportunities and took them. By 1920, for example, Andrew Casey, an Irish liquor dealer, had become a bank president and a hotel magnate. Michael Bosak, a Slovak immigrant who started life as a breaker boy in the 1880s, owned banks, a manufacturing company, and a real estate firm in Scranton in 1920. Few had the talent and vision to build such empires, but those who did picked up where the city's founders had left off.[54]

Scranton was, in a sense, America's first manufacturing city. It marked the spot where America began its independence from British iron. During the next generation, Scranton became a showcase of remarkable entrepreneurship and industrial growth. In this relatively open environment, Scranton's economic order was fluid: upward mobility for the poor existed side by side with downward mobility for the rich. Entrepreneurs were prize possessions for cities and for the nation; but their vision, talent, and drive were hard to transfer from generation to generation. Most of the families of Scranton's early industrialists died out as entrepreneurs; they didn't inherit their fathers' vision and turned over the city's economic leadership to newcomers.

And so the cycle goes—which means that if Scranton is typical, then two seemingly contradictory generalizations about the rise of big business are both true. First, a small constantly changing group of entrepreneurs consistently held a large share of the nation's wealth. Second, the poor didn't get poorer, and the rich didn't get richer either.

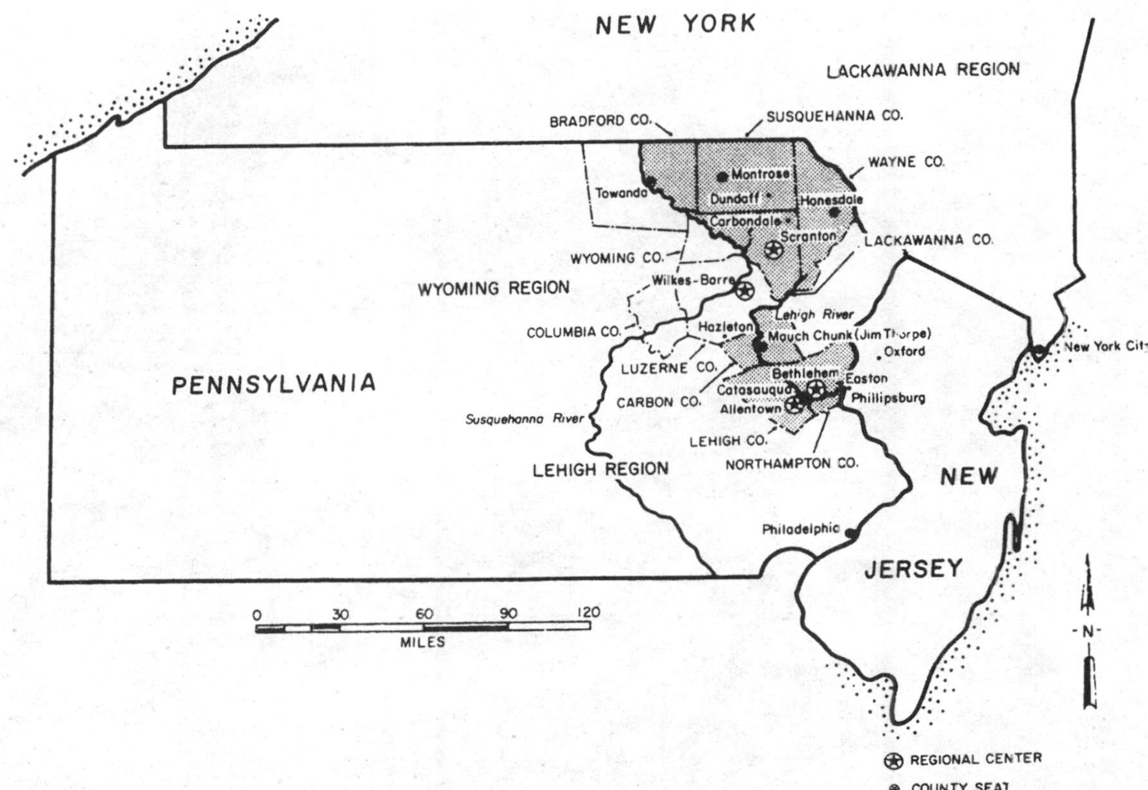

Map A. The Lackawanna, Wyoming, and Lehigh Regions

"The American spirit of conquest"

Courtesy Bethlehem Steel Corporation

The young Charles Schwab

CHAPTER FOUR

Charles Schwab and The Steel Industry

When asked for the secret of his success in the steel industry, Charles Schwab always talked about making the most with what you have, using praise, not criticism, giving liberal bonuses for work well done, and "appeal[ing] to the American spirit of conquest in my men, the spirit of doing things better than anyone has ever done them before." He liked to tell this story about how he handled an unproductive steel mill:

> I had a mill manager who was finely educated, thoroughly capable and master of every detail of the business. But he seemed unable to inspire his men to do their best.
>
> "How is it that a man as able as you," I asked him one day, "cannot make this mill turn out what it should?"
>
> "I don't know," he replied; "I have coaxed the men; I have pushed them, I have sworn at them. I have done everything in my power Yet they will not produce."
>
> It was near the end of the day; in a few minutes the night force would come on duty. I turned to a workman who was standing beside one of the red-mouthed furnaces and asked him for a piece of chalk.
>
> "How many heats has your shift made today?" I queried.
>
> "Six," he replied.
>
> I chalked a big "6" on the floor, and then passed along without another word. When the night shift came in they saw the "6" and asked about it.
>
> "The big boss was in here today," said the day men. "He asked us how many heats we had made, and we told him six. He chalked it down."
>
> The next morning I passed through the same mill. I saw that the "6" had been rubbed out and a big "7" written instead. The night shift

had announced itself. That night I went back. The "7" had been erased, and a "10" swaggered in its place.The day force recognized no superiors. Thus a fine competition was started, and it went on until this mill, formerly the poorest producer, was turning out more than any other mill in the plant.[1]

Schwab showed the ability to find solutions to problems even as a lad growing up in Loretto, Pennsylvania. According to one of his teachers, "Charlie was a boy who never said, 'I don't know.' He went on the principle of 'pretend that you know and if you don't, find out mighty quick'." Schwab knew early that he would have to live by his wits; his parents and immigrant grandparents weaved and traded wool products, jobs which put food on the table but not much money in the bank. Young Charlie, therefore, started work early in life: in one job he was a "singing cabby"; he drove passengers from nearby Cresson to Loretto and entertained them with ballads along the way. One of his passengers, impressed with the gregarious youth, gave him a travel book and Schwab later said, "It opened my eyes to the glories of the outside world, and stimulated my imagination tremendously." Soon, Loretto, Pennsylvania, population 300, would be too small to contain the ambitious Schwab. With his parents' blessing, he left home at age seventeen to clerk in a general store in Braddock, a suburb of Pittsburgh.[2]

Braddock was a steel town, varied in its cultural and urban life. Working in the store, young Charlie often pleased customers with his good looks, wit, and charm; one man whom he impressed was William "Captain Bill" Jones, the mill superintendent at Braddock for Carnegie Steel. Jones offered Schwab a place as a stake driver for the engineering corps who designed plans for building furnaces. Schwab accepted, proved himself capable, and soon became a draftsman. Here, he worked overtime to master his craft; within six months he became Jones' righthand man at the mill. As Jones' messenger boy, Schwab came into contact with the mill owner, the Scottish immigrant Andrew Carnegie. Carnegie took a special liking to Schwab, who wisely spent some of his off hours playing Scottish ballads on Carnegie's piano.[3]

Schwab worked hard to please Jones and Carnegie. Doing so allowed him to advance in the Carnegie organization. Fortunately for Schwab, Carnegie did not recruit his leaders on the basis of wealth or family standing. He used a merit system; he wanted people who could make the best steel possible at the lowest price. To succeed under Carnegie's system, Schwab would have to master the methods of steel production.

Carnegie stressed cutting costs: in fact his motto was "Watch the costs and the profits will take care of themselves." This meant hard work in innovating, accounting, and managing. Purchases, for example, were made in bulk to achieve economies of scale. Also, Carnegie strived for vertical integration, the control of his steel business from the buying of raw materials to the marketing of finished steel.[4]

At the heart of Carnegie's system were bonuses and partnerships for those who excelled. Strong incentives were given employees who could figure out how to save on iron ore, coke, and limestone; or how to produce a harder, cheaper steel; or how to capture new markets for steel. Carnegie explained that success "flows from having interested exceptional men in our service; thus only can we *develop ability* and hold it in our service." In fact, Carnegie said, "Every year should be marked by the promotion of one or more of our young men."[5]

Captain Jones had risen to mill superintendent this way. Among other things he had invented the Jones mixer, a device that cut costs in the transferring of steel from the blast furnace to the Bessemer converter. For his inventions and know-how, Carnegie paid him the highest salary in the business, $25,000—the same salary as that of the President of the United States.[6]

Schwab rose through the ranks just as Jones did. He completed small tasks and was given larger ones. At age twenty-three, he designed and built a bridge over the Baltimore and Ohio Railroad tracks; he saved time and money doing the job and received as a bonus ten $20 gold pieces from Carnegie himself. Other assignments followed: he installed meters in the factories and reduced waste of natural gas; he redesigned a rail-finishing department and saved ten cents per ton of steel; he effectively helped in calming down workers during a violent strike in the Homestead plant. When Captain Jones died in a blast furnace explosion in 1889, Schwab became the logical choice for superintendent at Braddock.[7]

Gregarious and competent, Schwab became Carnegie's problem solver. For example, the workers at Braddock were turning out "seconds," or substandard rails. Schwab's solution: give $20 cash bonuses to those steelmakers producing the fewest seconds. The quality of the rails shot up and the resulting increase in profits more than paid the bonuses given. No wonder that Carnegie soon gave Schwab a small partnership in Carnegie Steel, with the promise of more to come if he could keep producing. Carnegie even wrote one of his senior partners, Henry Clay Frick, that Schwab "gives every promise of being the man we have long desired" to eventually run the business.[8]

Schwab idolized Carnegie and found him amazing to watch. Carnegie's efficiency and his thorough knowledge of the industry made him a terror among fellow steel producers. He spied on them, used their annual reports against them, and even wrote them to secure information on costs of production. Meanwhile, Carnegie Steel was a closed corporation; he told outsiders nothing of his costs or his future plans. Carnegie disdained "pools," secret agreements among competitors to divide up the market and keep prices high. Pools were for the weak; Carnegie wanted to "scoop the market [and] run the mills full."[9]

Not that Carnegie didn't use friendships and other means to help him. In bidding on a large Union Pacific contract for rails, he may have outmaneuvered the veteran Scranton family. Joseph Scranton was a director on the Union Pacific as well as president of the Lackawanna Iron and Coal Company. But Carnegie had done a favor for Sidney Dillon, the president of the Union Pacific, and Dillon agreed to give Carnegie the contract if he would match the lowest bid.[10]

In the case of the Scrantons, Carnegie showed no mercy. When Carnegie went into the steel business in 1872, he was told that he could never compete against the Lackawanna Company; Joseph Scranton was a founding father of American rail-making; he had a generation of experience making rails. But that year Joseph Scranton died, and his sons William and Walter would be the ones to challenge Carnegie: first with the Lackawanna Company, then with their Scranton Steel Company. Carnegie and the Scrantons joined the Bessemer Steel Association in 1875, but their approaches were different: the Scrantons wanted a pool, but Carnegie told them and others that unless he got the largest share he would "withdraw from it and undersell you all in the market—and make good money doing it." The Scrantons and the others were bluffed by Carnegie and gave him his way. Carnegie then studied the Scrantons and learned their strengths and weaknesses. He discovered that they (and others) were discarding the thin steel shavings, called "scale," that fell on the floor when the steel passed through the rollers. When he learned this, he regularly sent a man to Scranton to cart away tons of the Scrantons' scale, almost free of charge, and brought it to Pittsburgh to use in making rails for Carnegie Steel.[11]

As Carnegie moved to the top of the American steel business, Schwab watched, learned, and proved himself time and again. In 1897 the thirty-five year old Schwab became president of Carnegie Steel and the two men ran the company together. Business was never better. Schwab put in sixteen new furnaces at the Homestead plant, and costs per ton of finished steel fell 34 percent in one year. To promote esprit de corps Schwab held Saturday meetings with all of his superintendents to work out problems. Meanwhile, the results of large-scale production took hold: the cost of making rails fell from $28 to $11.50 per ton from 1880 to 1900, but the profits from the larger volume of business went from $2 million in 1888 to $4 million in 1894, to $40 million in 1900. Some people wondered if Carnegie Steel might soon capture the steel trade of the entire world.[12]

Such speculating was premature. The next year, at age sixty-five, Carnegie retired and, with Schwab as his emissary, sold Carnegie Steel to J. P. Morgan for $480 million. Morgan then combined Carnegie Steel with other companies to create U. S. Steel, the first billion-dollar company in American history. The choice for president of the company: Charles Schwab.[13]

Reporters and critics condemned "The Steel Trust," as they called U. S. Steel, for its size and its potential to monopolize. Who would be able to compete, they asked, with such a large vertically integrated company? At his disposal, Schwab would have 213 steel mills and transportation companies, 41 iron ore mines, and 57,000 acres of coal land—enough, critics charged, to dwarf competitors and keep prices high.[14]

Schwab discovered, however, that he would not be able to use the Carnegie system at U. S. Steel. In fact, he would not have authority to run the company at all. Morgan and his friend Elbert Gary had organized U. S. Steel so that an executive committee, headed by Gary, and the board of directors would set the policies of the company; Schwab, as president, would carry them out. Morgan and Gary were interested in business stability, not in innovating or in cutting the price of steel. For example, when Schwab wanted to secure more ore land, Gary said no. He also opposed price-cutting, aggressive marketing, giving bonuses, and adopting new technology. Schwab later said, "Gary, who had no real knowledge of the steel business, forever opposed me on some of the methods and principles that I had seen worked out with Carnegie—methods that had made the Carnegie Company the most successful in the world."[15]

Schwab's personal life, more than disputes over policy, seems to have led to his downfall at U. S. Steel. He showed he had the values of a dissipater as well as those of an entrepreneur. When Carnegie was in control, Schwab consciously restrained his extravagant tastes; Carnegie deplored living beyond one's income, gambling, and adultery. But out from under Carnegie's grip, Schwab engaged in all three and almost ruined his marriage and his career. In New York City, Schwab built a gargantuan mansion, which consumed one whole block of the city and $7 million of his cash. He also gambled at Monte Carlo, which made bad newspaper copy and cost him credibility. Finally, he had an affair with a nurse, which resulted in a child. Though Schwab hid this from the press, he could not do so from his wife, Rana. The strain from his adultery, combined with the pressure of Monte Carlo, the expense of Riverside, and the barbs from Elbert Gary wrecked Schwab's health. He went to Europe to recover and, in 1904, resigned as president of U. S. Steel.[16]

Schwab, the man who said, "I cannot fail," seemed to have failed. He was depressed for months. Even Carnegie repudiated Schwab and this added to the pain. During his troubles he had insomnia, he lost weight, his arms and legs were regularly numb, and sometimes he fainted. His wife forgave him for his adultery and this no doubt eased the strain; but she was still not happy because she wanted a child of her own and never did have one. She didn't covet the extravagant life, so dear to her husband, and she spent many lonely days at Riverside.[17]

Schwab was out at U. S. Steel, but he already had the makings for a comeback. When he was president of U. S. Steel, Schwab had bought Bethlehem Steel as a private investment. He was criticized for this, especially when he merged Bethlehem Steel with some unsound companies into an unprofitable shipbuilding trust. This merger eventually collapsed; and when Schwab stepped down at U. S. Steel, he still had Bethlehem Steel as his own property. The demotion from being president of a company worth over one billion dollars, to being president of one worth less than nine million dollars, would have embarrassed some men, but not Schwab. He would have full control in running the company and would succeed or fail on his own abilities.[18]

Before Schwab took over Bethlehem Steel, its future had not looked promising. It had been founded in 1857 and soon produced rails for the Lehigh Valley Railroad. This was more than coincidence because entrepreneur Asa Packer, who had built the Lehigh Valley Railroad, held a large interest in what was then Bethlehem Iron. Packer, a Connecticut Yankee, had the vision and ability to promote both of these investments and make them profitable. His rise from carpenter to railroad tycoon had made him a legend in Pennsylvania; he was worth $17 million by the late 1870s. When he died in 1879, his sons, sons-in-law, and nephews took over his investments, but did not have the success that Packer did. The Lehigh Valley Railroad floundered and went into receivership in the Panic of 1893. Bethlehem Iron almost shared the same fate.[19]

Led by Philadelphians and the Packer group, Bethlehem Iron became very conservative after Packer's death. The younger leaders single-mindedly produced rails, even though (1) Carnegie was doing it cheaper, and (2) they had the expense of importing most of their iron ore from Cuba. They escaped a price squeeze in 1885 when, reluctantly, they shifted from making rails to making military ordnance, which commanded a higher price per ton than rails. Such an imaginative strategy, as one might expect, did not originate within the Packer group; in fact, they resisted it until declining profits on rails presented them with no alternative.[20]

The wise, if belated, switch from rails to gun-forgings and armor plate led to profits because Bethlehem Iron was the only bidder on its first government contract for ordnance in 1887. Other contracts were forthcoming and Bethlehem Iron "established a reputation for quality and reliability," if not for aggressiveness and efficiency. Regarding the last, its operations were so inefficient that the company in 1898 hired Frederick W. Taylor, master of scientific management, to suggest ways of improving worker productivity. Yet the Packer group soon became hostile to Taylor's cost-cutting ideas. Of one suggestion to reduce the number of workers handling raw materials, Taylor observed that the owners "did not wish me, as they said, to depopulate South Bethlehem." He further commented, "They owned all the houses in South Bethlehem and the company stores, and when they saw we [Taylor and his assistants] were cutting the labor force down to about one-fourth, they did not want it." They also rejected Taylor's suggestions to standardize job functions and give raises to key personnel.[21]

Surviving, then, on government contracts, Bethlehem Iron stumbled into the twentieth century—a profitable operation in spite of itself. In the midst of this conservatism, Schwab came to Bethlehem in 1904 and boldly announced that he would "make the Bethlehem plant the greatest armor plate and gun factory in the world." Taking the helm, Schwab "backed Bethlehem with every dollar I could borrow." This backing included buying new branch plants and closing unprofitable ones, getting new contracts by selling aggressively, and reorganizing the company as Bethlehem Steel. Planning for the future, Schwab bought large tracts of land for the company east of South Bethlehem. He also bought or leased more ore land and mechanized the company's Cuban iron fields to spur production there.[22]

Schwab's entrepreneurship clashed with the Packer group's cautiousness right from the start. As one historian said, "Many of the veteran Bethlehem executives preferred the old, pre-Taylor and pre-Schwab way of doing things. They resented Schwab; he was an intruder." Soon after arriving in South Bethlehem, Schwab ousted the inbred Packer group from authority. In the new president's remarkable words, "I selected fifteen young men right out of the mill and made them my partners." Two of these "partners" were Eugene Grace, the son of a sea captain, and Archibald Johnston, a local Moravian. They later became presidents of Bethlehem Steel.[23]

After reorganization Schwab wanted to diversify his company and challenge U. S. Steel. To do this, he began making rails and moving Bethlehem Steel away from its dependence on government contracts. Schwab adopted open-hearth technology because it produced better rails than the Bessemer system did. As historian Robert Hessen notes:

> U. S. Steel, the nation's largest rail producer, did not follow Schwab's lead; it would have had to replace its Bessemer facilities with open hearth equipment. Being a late starter, Bethlehem enjoyed a clear advantage: with no heavy investment in obsolete equipment to protect, it could adopt the newest and most efficient technological processes.[24]

Schwab's reorganization of the Cuban ore mines also improved Bethlehem's competitive position at the expense of U. S. Steel.

Cuban ore was richer in iron and lower in phosphorus than was the Mesabi range ore used by U. S. Steel. It also had another advantage: it contained large amounts of nickel, so that Bethlehem could produce nickel steel at no extra cost. For a ton of iron Bethlehem's cost was $4.31; U. S. Steel's was $7.10.[25]

Now that Schwab was running an efficient diversified company he turned his attention to cutting costs. He reasoned that workers would work harder if they knew it would directly result in a raise. Therefore, he set up a bonus system for productive laborers, foremen, and managers throughout the company. As Schwab described it, "Do so much and you get so much; do more and you get more—that is the essence of the system." At U.S. Steel, by contrast, Gary tied bonuses to the overall profitability of the company, not to individual performance. Under that system, Schwab noted, a worker could toil hard and creatively and receive no reward.[26]

Schwab wanted bursts of creative energy and he paid the highest salaries in the industry to get them. When Eugene Grace proved himself, Schwab made him president of the company, regularly paying him salary and bonuses of over one million dollars per year. This was twice as much as Gary earned at U.S. Steel. Gary could never understand Schwab's philosophy of cutting costs. It didn't seem logical to pay bonuses in order to lower expenses and increase profits. But Schwab showed that this worked, and Bethlehem Steel's sales grew from $10 million in 1904 to $230 million in 1916. During these same years, the company's stock increased in value from $20 to $600 per share.[27]

Schwab's biggest move at Bethlehem was his challenge to U.S. Steel in the making of structural steel. Here he focused on an innovation in making the steel beams that went into bridges and skyscrapers. Schwab had been listening to Edward Grey, who had an idea of making steel beams directly from an ingot as a single section instead of riveting smaller beams together. Grey claimed that his invention provided "the greatest possible strength with the least dead weight and at the lowest cost."[28]

The other steelmakers rejected Grey's theory; but Schwab was eager to try it even though it would cost $5 million to design the plant, build the mill, and pay Grey's royalties. The problem was that the experts were so skeptical that Schwab had trouble raising money. In fact, he almost backed out but then jumped back in with the

The Bettmann Archive

Carnegie: "Watch the costs and the profits will take care of themselves."

statement: "If we are going bust, we will go bust big." He staked his own money, and that of his company, on the Grey beam, but still he needed more. So Schwab buttonholed wealthy investors for large personal loans and then, through remarkable salesmanship, persuaded his major suppliers, the Lehigh Valley and the Reading Railroads, to give him credit on deliveries of the new steel. Schwab then aggressively recruited big contracts for the "Bethlehem beam": the Chase National Bank and the Metropolitan Life Insurance Company in New York were among them. The experiment worked. This cheaper and more durable beam quickly became Schwab's greatest innovation and he captured a large share of the structural steel market from U. S. Steel.[29]

Schwab's actions had consequences for the American steel industry. From 1905 to 1920, Bethlehem Steel's labor force doubled every five years. By contrast, U. S. Steel often stagnated; one officer noted after Schwab left that "works standing idle have deteriorated ... the men are disheartened and a certain amount of apathy exists." By the 1920s, the chagrined leaders at U. S. Steel secretly began making Bethlehem beams; as an official there observed, "The tonnage lost on account of competition with Bethlehem ... is ... ever increasing.... We are obliged to sell...at unusually low prices in order to compete." Schwab discovered their ploy, however, and forced U. S. Steel to pay him royalties for making his Bethlehem beams.[30]

Schwab had transformed Bethlehem Steel. Even before World War I his company had become the second largest steelmaker in America. The *New York Times* praised Bethlehem Steel as "possibly the most efficient, profitable self-contained steel plant in the country." By 1920, it employed 20,000 people in the Lehigh Valley and was among the largest enterprises in the world. In 1922, it absorbed Lackawanna Steel, the company that launched America's rail-making industry seventy-five years earlier.[31]

During World War I, Schwab's abilities were needed by the U. S. government. In April, 1918, one year after America entered the war, victory was uncertain. Delays in shipping cargo and troops from America to Europe threatened the Allies with defeat. More ships were needed; but in the U.S. shipyards few ships were forthcoming. Within the Wilson administration some blamed the owners of the shipyards; others blamed the workers; still others blamed radical unions. In the midst of this fingerpointing, Franklin K. Lane, the Secretary of Commerce, posed a solution:

> The President ought to send for Schwab and hand him a treasury warrant for a billion dollars and set him to work building ships, with no government inspectors or supervisors or accountants or auditors or other red tape to bother him. Let the President just put it up to Schwab's patriotism and put Schwab on his honor. Nothing more is needed. Schwab will do the job.

That month Schwab became Director-General of the Emergency Fleet Corporation for the U. S. government. In his investigation, he discovered cases of laziness, incompetence, work slowdowns, and poor coordination of the ship building. As usual, though, Schwab said, "The best place to succeed is where you are with what you have." He quickly rearranged incentives: he eliminated the "cost plus" system whereby shipyards were paid whatever it cost them to build ships plus a percentage of that as a profit. Instead, Schwab tied profits to cost-cutting by paying a set price per ship. Cost overruns would be paid by the shipbuilders who would have to be efficient to make a profit. As usual, bonuses were part of the Schwab formula. He paid them, sometimes out of his own pocket, to those shipbuilders who exceeded production.[32]

Schwab enjoyed being a showman, so he went to the shipyards himself: he rallied the workers, praised the owners, and even drew applause in a speech to the Industrial Workers of the World, a radical union. Never one to ignore symbols for achievement, Schwab had Rear Admiral F. F. Fletcher head a group to award flags and medals to plants and workers whose work had been outstanding. By the fall of 1918, ships were being completed on time and even ahead of schedule. President Wilson and the leaders of the Shipping Board were astonished with the change and gave Schwab the credit. Carnegie, in the last year of his life, called it "a record of accomplishment such as has never been equaled."[33]

Not all of Schwab's dealings with the federal government were so productive. The armor-plate business is an example of this. The making of military equipment—armor plate for ships, gun forgings, ordnance, and shrapnel—brought Schwab into regular contact with government purchasers. Throughout his career, Schwab had problems with these government contracts. Even at Carnegie Steel, Schwab had quarreled with government officials over allegedly defective armor plate; the issue never was amicably settled.[34]

The problem began in the 1880s when various officials began urging the United States to build a large Navy. At the time the

American steel companies were mostly making rails, so President Cleveland and others began urging someone to diversify. Making military equipment was complicated and expensive, however; only reluctantly did Bethlehem Iron and Carnegie Steel shift into ordnance. Had the government not promised them Navy contracts they would not have switched.[35]

Four things in the military supply business made for tension between the federal government and the steel companies. First, the federal government was the largest and sometimes the only buyer of military equipment; the government's notions of quality sometimes differed from that of the producers. Often both sides had legitimate points of view. Second, since the demand for military equipment was limited and the costs of building a factory to produce it were high, only U. S. Steel, Bethlehem Steel, and later Midvale Steel made armor plate. The potential for either a monoply or for price-rigging bothered some government officials. Third, a ton of military equipment was more expensive to make than a ton of rails or a ton of structural steel; some purchasers thought that $450 for a ton of armor plate was price-gouging if rails sold for only $25 per ton. Finally, the ordnance producers sometimes made lower bids on foreign contracts than they did on domestic ones. To some in the American government, this was evidence they were being overcharged; to the steel companies, lower bids meant they had to cut their profit margin to almost zero to overcome tariffs in foreign countries. Also, when American needs were low, the steel men argued they had to get foreign business to keep their factories operating.[36]

The government's solution to these four problems was to threaten to go into the military supply business and build an armor-plate factory with federal funds. Schwab countered that the government would not be able to make armor plate cheaper than he could. After all, Bethlehem had a veteran work force, a good bonus system, and could buy materials more cheaply in bulk. Any vertically integrated company would have an advantage over companies purchasing supplies in the open market. A government factory, Schwab insisted, would waste the taxpayers' money.[37]

If Schwab had been a mediator, not a participant, he might have been able to settle this dispute. Part of the problem was the same as that of the low productivity of the American shipyards during World War I: misdirected incentives. When the Navy department took bids for contracts from the three steel companies, it naturally accepted the lowest bid. But then the Navy official went to the two higher bidders and offered them part of the contract if they would agree to accept the lowest bid. He did this so that all three could survive; that way, with three producers, a future monopoly of ordnance would be prevented. The problem is that this strategy gave the three companies an incentive to collude and fix prices high. Why should they bid low if all of them would get part of the contract anyway? A winner-take-all approach would have provided an incentive for lower bidding, but the Navy department was unwilling to do this. Not surprisingly, then, year after year the steel companies submitted nearly identical bids for military equipment.[38]

This problem reached a crisis point during the Wilson administration. In 1913, Josephus Daniels, Wilson's Secretary of the Navy, and Ben Tillman, Senator from South Carolina, investigated the armor business. Both men urged Wilson to back a government armor plant. They held hearings in Congress on the armor business but did not like what they heard. The leaders of the three steel companies all said their bids were reasonable. In fact, Schwab submitted figures showing that he and the others charged less for armor plate than did England, France, Germany and Japan. If others didn't believe it, then let the Federal Trade Commission look at the accounts and fix a price. Daniels and Tillman rejected this. They were convinced that the government could make armor plate cheaper. The head of the Bureau of Ordnance estimated that $10.3 million would build an armor plant and that plate could be made for less than $300 per ton, instead of $454 per ton, which was a typical bid from the steel companies.[39]

In 1916, then, Daniels and Tillman began the campaign to convince Congress to spend $11 million for an armor factory. In the Senate, Tillman argued that the government would save money and would no longer be at the mercy of identical bids from the "greedy and hoggish" steel companies. President Wilson backed Tillman and said, "I remember very well my promise to help all I could with the bill for the construction of an armor plant and I stand ready to redeem my promise."[40]

Schwab led the effort to defeat the bill. He spoke out against it in public and ran ads in over 3,000 newspapers challenging the need for a government plant. He stressed the fairness angle. He said that years ago the government had asked Bethlehem to make armor; they had done so only when the government agreed to buy from them.

Now, with $7 million invested in equipment, the government was planning to build its own plant and make Bethlehem's useless.[41]

Most Congressmen, however, bought the arguments of Tillman and Daniels. The bill passed the Senate and the House by about two to one margins, and Wilson signed it. As Senator Albert Cummins of Iowa said, "It is [one of] my profoundest convictions that the manufacture of armor-plate for battleships is a government function. I hope the private enterprises will be entirely eliminated."[42]

Dozens of cities lobbied to be the site for the new plant. From Rome, Georgia, to Kalamazoo, Michigan, city after city was put forth as being uniquely situated to produce armor plate. The winner of this competition was South Charleston, West Virginia. Congress soon raised the appropriation to $17.5 million and authorized the South Charleston plant to make guns and projectiles, as well as armor. Construction began in 1917 on the new factory and on hundreds of houses for the workers. The war delayed the building, but it was continued later. Higher construction costs after the war meant an overrun of several million dollars. By 1921, the new plant was making guns, projectiles, and armor—all at prices apparently much higher than that of Bethlehem Steel. Within a year the whole plant was shut down, put on "inoperative status," and never run again.[43]

Schwab turned sixty in 1921 and was beginning to look backward more than forward. There was much to see: whether he had made rails, beams, or armor plate, he was successful. Even Carnegie, near death, had recently written Schwab, "I have never doubted your ability to triumph in anything you undertook. I cannot help feeling proud of you for having far outstripped any of my 'boys'."[44]

In the 1920s and 1930s, however, Schwab seemed to lose his entrepreneurial spirit. Producing a better product at a lower price no longer seemed to dominate his thinking. Let's "live and let live," Schwab told the steelmakers at the American Iron and Steel Institute in 1927. Next year, he urged them to fix prices and avoid cutting them. The year after this, Schwab, the father of the Bethlehem beam, urged the steel men not to expand but to use their existing plant capacity.[45]

When the Great Depression took hold in the 1930s, Schwab's public addresses were full of anecdotes and preaching that "the good. . .lies ahead." One of Schwab's remedies for the ailing economy was a high protective tariff. He had always favored a tariff on imported steel but usually settled for low duties. The Smoot-Hawley

Courtesy Bethlehem Steel Corporation

Charles Schwab: backed Bethlehem Steel with every dollar he could borrow.

Tariff of 1930 created the highest duties in American history on many items. Some writers have argued that the Smoot-Hawley Tariff triggered the Great Depression; others say it merely made the depression worse. One thing is certain: many nations retaliated against high American tariffs by closing off their borders to American-made goods. The demand for American goods, therefore, declined and this put more people out of work. When Cordell Hull, Roosevelt's Secretary of State, tried to lower American tariffs in 1934, Schwab opposed it. He was afraid of foreign competition.[46]

During the 1930s, Schwab enjoyed his role as elder statesman of the steel industry. He was full of stories and ever ready to do interviews with reporters. He never got senile; his ability to memorize speeches and his knack for remembering names and faces was still amazing. He just preferred to let Eugene Grace and others run Bethlehem Steel, while he worked the crowd.[47]

When Schwab retired as an entrepreneur, his fortune became jeopardized. He had earlier shown the traits of a dissipater and had the potential to run through his $25 million fortune. Liberated from work, Schwab traveled, gambled, and flirted more than ever. He joined the New York Whist Club and played there for high stakes. He frequented the roulette tables in Monte Carlo with his favorite mistress. The art of speculation, an anathema to Carnegie, appealed to Schwab: he installed a ticker tape in his mansion to keep tabs on Wall Street; he also invested in a variety of companies and knew almost nothing about some of them. Gambling wasn't the only drain on Schwab's wealth: he co-signed one million dollars worth of notes—usually worthless—for "friends" and also gave monthly allowances to twenty-seven people.[48]

Schwab refused to cut back on expenses, even during the Great Depression. He still hired the most famous musicians of the era to give private recitals for him at Riverside. The mansion itself—complete with swimming pool, wine cellar, gymnasium, bowling alley, six elevators, and ninety bedrooms—needed twenty servants to keep it functioning. He also hired 300 men to care for his 1000-acre estate at Loretto. So Schwab desperately needed his $250,000 annual salary at Bethlehem, given for past services, just to pay his expenses. From 1935 to 1938, a small group of rebel stockholders attended the company's annual meetings; they challenged Schwab's salary and told him he had "outlived his usefulness." He finally stopped them by privately telling one of the critics that he desperately needed the money to live on. Actually he needed more. He couldn't pay the annual taxes on Riverside and couldn't sell it either, even at a $6 million loss. He couldn't even give it away, when he offered it as the residence for the mayor.[49]

Schwab's last years were also marked by poor health and the death of his wife, who had borne him no children. After her funeral, Riverside was taken by creditors; Schwab moved into a small apartment. Schwab, who had shown the world a vision of entrepreneurship, now had only a vision of death. "A man knows when he doesn't want to be alive," he said, "when the will to continue living has gone from him." Schwab died nine months after he said this, at age seventy-seven with debts exceeding assets by over $300,000.[50]

"Refining oil for the poor man"

Rockefeller Archives Center

John D. Rockefeller, in his mid-twenties.

CHAPTER FIVE

John D. Rockefeller and the Oil Industry

In 1885 John D. Rockefeller wrote one of his partners, "Let the good work go on. We must ever remember we are refining oil for the poor man and he must have it cheap and good." Or as he put it to another partner: "Hope we can continue to hold out with the best illuminator in the world at the *lowest* price." Even after twenty years in the oil business, "the best. . .at the lowest price" was still Rockefeller's goal; his Standard Oil Company had already captured 90 percent of America's oil refining and had pushed the price down from 58 cents to eight cents a gallon. His well-groomed horses delivered blue barrels of oil throughout America's cities and were already symbols of excellence and efficiency. Consumers were not only choosing Standard Oil over that of his competitors; they were also preferring it to coal oil, whale oil, and electricity. Millions of Americans illuminated their homes with Standard Oil for one cent per hour; and in doing so, they made Rockefeller the wealthiest man in American history.[1]

Rockefeller's early life hardly seemed the making of a near billionaire. His father was a peddler who often struggled to make ends meet. His mother stayed at home to raise their six children. They moved around upstate New York—from Richford to Moravia to Owego—and eventually settled in Cleveland, Ohio. John D. was the oldest son. Although he didn't have new suits or a fashionable home, his family life was stable. From his father he learned how to earn money and hold on to it; from his mother he learned to put God first in his life, to be honest, and help others.[2]

"From the beginning," Rockefeller said, "I was trained to work, to save, and to give." He did all three of these things shortly after he graduated from the Cleveland public high school. He always remembered the "momentous day" in 1855, when he began work at age sixteen as an assistant bookkeeper for 50 cents per day.[3]

On the job Rockefeller had a fixation for honest business. He later said, "I had learned the underlying principles of business as well as many men acquire them by the time they are forty." His first partner, Maurice Clark, said that Rockefeller "was methodical to an extreme, careful as to details and exacting to a fraction. If there was a cent due us he wanted it. If there was a cent due a customer he wanted the customer to have it." Such precision irritated some debtors, but it won him the confidence of many Cleveland businessmen; at age nineteen Rockefeller went into the grain shipping business on Lake Erie and soon began dealing in thousands of dollars.[4]

Rockefeller so enjoyed business that he dreamed about it at night. Where he really felt at ease, though, was with his family and at church. His wife Laura was also a strong Christian and they spent many hours a week attending church services, picnics, or socials at the Erie Street Baptist Church. Rockefeller saw a strong spiritual life as crucial to an effective business life. He tithed from his first paycheck and gave to his church, a foreign mission, and the poor. He sought Christians as business partners and later as employees. One of his fellow churchmen, Samuel Andrews, was investing in oil refining; and this new frontier appealed to young John. He joined forces with Andrews in 1865 and would apply his same precision and honesty to the booming oil industry.[5]

The discovery of large quantities of crude oil in northwest Pennsylvania soon changed the lives of millions of Americans. For centuries, people had known of the existence of crude oil scattered about America and the world. They just didn't know what to do with it. Farmers thought it a nuisance and tried to plow around it; others bottled it and sold it as medicine.[6]

In 1855, Benjamin Silliman, Jr., a professor of chemistry at Yale, analyzed a batch of crude oil; after distilling and purifying it, he found that it yielded kerosene—a better illuminant than the popular whale oil. Other by-products of distilling included lubricating oil, gasoline, and paraffin, which made excellent candles. The only problem was cost: it was too expensive to haul the small deposits of crude from northwest Pennsylvania to markets elsewhere. Silliman and others, however, formed an oil company and sent "Colonel" Edwin L. Drake, a jovial railroad conductor, to Titusville to drill for oil.

"Nonsense," said local skeptics. "You can't pump oil out of the ground as you pump water." Drake had faith that he could; in 1859, when he built a thirty-foot derrick and drilled seventy feet into the ground, all the locals scoffed. When he hit oil, however, they quickly converted and preached oil drilling as the salvation of the region. There were few barriers to entering the oil business: drilling equipment cost less than $1,000, and oil land seemed abundant. By the early 1860s, speculators were swarming northwest Pennsylvania, cluttering it with derricks, pipes, tanks, and barrels. "A good time coming for whales," concluded one newspaper. America had become hooked on kerosene.

Cleveland was a mere hundred miles from the oil region, and Rockefeller was fascinated with the prospects of refining oil into kerosene. He may have visited the region as early as 1862. By 1863 he was talking oil with Samuel Andrews and two years later they built a refinery together. Two things about the oil industry, however, bothered Rockefeller right from the start: the appalling waste and the fluctuating prices.

The overproducing of oil and the developing of new markets caused the price of oil to fluctuate wildly. In 1862 a barrel (42 gallons) of oil dropped in value from $4.00 to $.35. Later, when President Lincoln bought oil to fight the Civil War, the price jumped back to $4.00, then to $13.75. A blacksmith took $200 worth of drilling equipment and drilled a well worth $100,000. Others, with better drills and richer holes, dug four wells worth $200,000. Alongside the new millionaires of the moment were the thousands of fortune hunters who came from all over to lease land and kick down shafts into it with cheap foot drills. Most failed. Even Colonel Drake died in poverty. As J. W. Trowbridge wrote, "Almost everybody you meet has been suddenly enriched or suddenly ruined (perhaps both within a short space of time), or knows plenty of people who have."[7]

Those few who struck oil often wasted more than they earned. Thousands of barrels of oil poured into Oil Creek, not into tanks. Local creek bottoms were often flooded with runaway oil; the Allegheny River smelled of oil and glistened with it for many miles toward Pittsburgh. Gushers of wasted oil were bad enough; sometimes a careless smoker would turn a spouting well into a killing inferno. Other wasters would torpedo holes with nitroglycerine, sometimes losing the oil and their lives.[8]

Rockefeller was intrigued with the future of the oil industry, but was repelled by its past. He shunned the drills and derricks and chose the refining end instead. Refining eventually became very costly, but in the 1860s the main supplies were only barrels, a trough, a tank, and a still in which to boil the oil. The yield would usually be about 60 percent kerosene, 10 percent gasoline, 5 to 10 percent benzol or naphtha, with the rest being tar and wastes. High prices and dreams of quick riches brought many into refining; and this attracted Rockefeller, too. But right from the start, he believed that the path to success was to cut waste and produce the best product at the lowest price. Sam Andrews, his partner, worked on getting more kerosene per barrel of crude. Both men searched for uses for the by-products: they used the gasoline for fuel, some of the tars for paving, and shipped the naphtha to gas plants. They also sold lubricating oil, vaseline, and paraffin for making candles. Other Cleveland refiners, by contrast, were wasteful: they dumped their gasoline into the Cuyahoga River, they threw out other by-products, and they spilled oil throughout the city.[9]

Rockefeller was constantly looking for ways to save. For example, he built his refineries well and bought no insurance. He also employed his own plumber and almost halved the cost on labor, pipes, and plumbing materials. Coopers charged $2.50 per barrel; Rockefeller cut this to $.96 when he bought his own tracts of white oak timber, his own kilns to dry the wood, and his own wagons and horses to haul it to Cleveland. There with machines he made the barrels, then hooped them, glued them, and painted them blue. Rockefeller and Andrews soon became the largest refiners in Cleveland. In 1870, they reorganized with Rockefeller's brother William, and Henry Flagler, the son of a Presbyterian minister. They renamed their enterprise Standard Oil.[10]

Under Rockefeller's leadership they plowed the profits into bigger and better equipment; and, as their volume increased, they hired chemists and developed three hundred by-products from each barrel of oil. They ranged from paint and varnish to dozens of lubricating oils to anesthetics. As for the main product, kerosene, Rockefeller made it so cheaply that whale oil, coal oil, and, for a while, electricity lost out in the race to light American homes, factories, and streets. "We had vision," Rockefeller later said. "We saw the vast possibilities of the oil industry, stood at the center of it, and brought our knowledge and imagination and business experience to bear in a dozen, in twenty, in thirty directions."[11]

Another area of savings came from rebates from railroads. The major eastern railroads—the New York Central, the Erie, and Pennsylvania—all wanted to ship oil and were willing to give discounts, or rebates, to large shippers. These rebates were customary and dated back to the first shipments of oil. As the largest oil refiner in America, Rockefeller was in a good position to save money for himself and for the railroad as well. He promised to ship 60 carloads of oil daily and provide all the loading and unloading services. All the railroads had to do was to ship it east. Commodore Vanderbilt of the New York Central was delighted to give Rockefeller the largest rebate he gave any shipper for the chance to have the most regular, quick and efficient deliveries. When smaller oil men screamed about rate discrimination, Vanderbilt's spokesmen gladly promised the same rebate to anyone else who would give him the same volume of business. Since no other refiner was as efficient as Rockefeller, no one else got Standard Oil's discount.[12]

Many of Rockefeller's competitors condemned him for receiving such large rebates. But Rockefeller would never have gotten them had he not been the largest shipper of oil. These rebates, on top of his remarkable efficiency, meant that most refiners could not compete. From 1865 to 1870, the price of kerosene dropped from 58 to 26 cents per gallon. Rockefeller made profits during every one of these years, but most of Cleveland's refiners disappeared. Naturally, there were hard feelings. Henry Demarest Lloyd, whose cousin was an unhappy oil man, wrote *Wealth Against Commonwealth* in 1894 to denounce Rockefeller. Ida Tarbell, whose father was a Pennsylvania oil producer, attacked Rockefeller in a series of articles for *McClure's* magazine.[13]

Some of the oil producers were unhappy, but American consumers were pleased that Rockefeller was selling cheap oil. Before 1870, only the rich could afford whale oil and candles. The rest had to go to bed early to save money. By the 1870s, with the drop in the price of kerosene, middle and working class people all over the nation could afford the one cent an hour that it cost to light their homes at night. Working and reading became after-dark activities new to most Americans in the 1870s.[14]

Rockefeller quickly learned that he couldn't please everyone by making cheap oil. He pleased no one, though, when he briefly turned to political entrepreneurship in 1872. He joined a pool called the South Improvement Company and it turned out to be one of the biggest mistakes in his life. This scheme was hatched by Tom Scott of the Pennsylvania Railroad. Scott was nervous about low oil prices and falling railroad rates. He thought that if the large refiners and railroads got together they could artificially fix high prices for themselves. Rockefeller decided to join because he would get not only large rebates, but also drawbacks, which were discounts on that oil which his competitors, not he, shipped. The small producers and refiners bitterly attacked Rockefeller and forced the Pennsylvania Legislature to revoke the charter of the South Improvement Company. No oil was ever shipped under this pool, but Rockefeller got bad publicity from it and later admitted that he had been wrong.[15]

At first, the idea of a pool appealed to Rockefeller because it might stop the glut, the waste, the inefficiency, and the fluctuating prices of oil. The South Improvement Company showed him that this would not work, so he turned to market entrepreneurship instead. He decided to become the biggest and best refiner in the world. First, he put his chemists to work trying to extract even more from each barrel of crude. More important, he tried to integrate Standard Oil vertically and horizontally by getting dozens of other refiners to join him. Rockefeller bought their plants and talent; he gave the owners cash or stock in Standard Oil.[16]

From Rockefeller's standpoint, a few large vertically integrated oil companies could survive and prosper, but dozens of smaller companies could not. Improve or perish was Rockefeller's approach. "We will take your burdens," Rockefeller said. "We will utilize your ability; we will give you representation; we will all unite together and build a substantial structure on the basis of cooperation." Many oil men rejected Rockefeller's offer, but dozens of others all over America sold out to Standard Oil. When they did, Rockefeller simply shut down the inefficient companies and used what he needed from the good ones. Officers Oliver Payne, H. H. Rogers, and President John Archbold came to Standard Oil from these merged firms.[17]

Buying out competitors was a tricky business. Rockefeller's approach was to pay what the property was worth at the time he bought it. Outmoded equipment was worth little, but good personnel and even good will were worth a lot. Rockefeller had a tendency to be generous because he wanted the future good will of his new partners and employees. "He treated everybody fairly," concluded one oil man. "When we sold out he gave us a fair price. Some refiners tried to impose on him and when they found they could not do it, they abused him. I remember one man whose refinery was worth $6,000, or at most $8,000. His friends told him, 'Mr. Rockefeller ought to give you $100,000 for that.' Of course, Mr. Rockefeller refused to pay more than the refinery was worth, and the man . . . abused Mr. Rockefeller."[18]

Bigness was not Rockefeller's real goal. It was just a means of cutting costs. During the 1870s, the price of kerosene dropped from 26 to eight cents a gallon and Rockefeller captured about 90 percent of the American market. This percentage remained steady for years. Rockefeller never wanted to oust all of his rivals, just the ones who were wasteful and those who tarnished the whole trade by selling defective oil. "Competitors we must have, we must have," said Rockefeller's partner Charles Pratt. "If we absorb them, be sure it will bring up another."[19]

Just as Rockefeller reached the top, many predicted his demise. During the early 1880s, the entire oil industry was in jeopardy. The Pennsylvania oil fields were running dry and electricity was beginning to compete with lamps for lighting homes. No one knew about the oil fields out west and few suspected that the gasoline engine would be made the power source of the future. Meanwhile, the Russians had begun drilling and selling their abundant oil, and they raced to capture Standard Oil's foreign markets. Some experts predicted the imminent death of the American oil industry; even Standard Oil's loyal officers began selling some of their stock.[20]

Rockefeller's solution to these problems was to stake the future of his company on new oil discoveries near Lima, Ohio. Drillers found oil in this Ohio-Indiana region in 1885, but they could not market it. It had a sulphur base and stank like rotten eggs. Even touching this oil meant a long, soapy bath or social ostracism. No one wanted to sell or buy it and no city even wanted it shipped there. Only Rockefeller seemed interested in it. According to Joseph Seep, chief oil buyer for Standard Oil,

> Mr. Rockefeller went on buying leases in the Lima field in spite of the coolness of the rest of the directors, until he had accumulated more than 40 million barrels of that sulphurous oil in tanks. He must have

invested millions of dollars in buying and storing and holding the sour oil for two years, when everyone else thought it was no good.[21]

Rockefeller had hired two chemists, Herman Frasch and William Burton, to figure out how to purify the oil; he counted on them to make it usable. Rockefeller's partners were skeptical, however, and sought to stanch the flood of money invested in tanks, pipelines, and land in the Lima area. They "held up their hands in holy horror" at Rockefeller's gamble and even outvoted him at a meeting of Standard's Board of Directors. "Very well, gentlemen," said Rockefeller. "At my own personal risk, I will put up the money to care for this product: $2 million—$3 million, if necessary." Rockefeller told what then happened:

> This ended the discussion, and we carried the Board with us and continued to use the funds of the company in what was regarded as a very hazardous investment of money. But we persevered, and two or three of our practical men stood firmly with me and constantly occupied themselves with the chemists until at last, after millions of dollars had been expended in the tankage and buying the oil and constructing the pipelines and tank cars to draw it away to the markets where we could sell it for fuel, one of our German chemists cried 'Eureka!' We . . . at last found ourselves able to clarify the oil.[22]

The "worthless" Lima oil that Rockefeller had stockpiled suddenly became valuable; Standard Oil would be able to supply cheap kerosene for years to come. Rockefeller's exploit had come none too soon: the Russians struck oil at Baku, four square miles of the deepest and richest oil land in the world. They hired European experts to help Russia conquer the oil markets of the world. In 1882, the year before Baku oil was first exported, America refined 85 percent of the world's oil; six years later this dropped to 53 percent. Since most of Standard's oil was exported, and since Standard accounted for 90 percent of America's exported oil, the Baku threat had to be met.[23]

At first glance, Standard Oil seemed certain to lose. First, the Baku oil was centralized in one small area: this made it economical to drill, refine, and ship from a single location. Second, the Baku oil was more plentiful: its average yield was over 280 barrels per well per day, compared with 4.5 barrels per day from American wells. Third, Baku oil was highly viscous: it made a better lubricant (though not necessarily a better illuminant) than oil in Pennsylvania or Ohio. Fourth, Russia was closer to European and Asian markets: Standard

Oil had to bear the costs of building huge tankers and crossing the ocean with them. One independent expert estimated that Russia's costs of oil exporting were one-third to one-half of those of the United States. Finally, Russia and other countries slapped high protective tariffs on American oil; this allowed inefficient foreign drillers to compete with Standard Oil. The Austro-Hungarian empire, for example, imported over half a million barrels of American oil in 1882; but they bought none by 1890. What was worse, local refiners there marketed a low-grade oil in barrels labeled "Standard Oil Company." This allowed the Austro-Hungarians to dump their cheap oil and damage Standard's reputation at the same time.

Rockefeller pulled out all stops to meet the Russian challenge. No small refinery would have had a chance; even a large vertically integrated company like Standard Oil was at a great disadvantage. Rockefeller never lost his vision, though, of conquering the oil markets of the world. First, he relied on his research team to help him out. William Burton, who helped clarify the Lima oil, invented "cracking," a method of heating oil to higher temperatures to get more use of the product out of each barrel. Engineers at Standard Oil helped by perfecting large steamship tankers, which cut down on the costs of shipping oil overseas.

Second, Rockefeller made Standard Oil even more efficient. He used less iron in making barrel hoops and less solder in sealing oil cans. In a classic move, he used the waste (culm) from coal heaps to fuel his refineries; even the sweepings from his factory he sorted through for tin shavings and solder drops.

Third, Rockefeller studied the foreign markets and learned how to beat the Russians in their part of the world. He sent Standard agents into dozens of countries to figure out how to sell oil up the Hwang Ho River in China, along the North Road in India, to the east coast of Sumatra, and to the huts of tribal chieftains in Malaya. He even used spies, often foreign dipomats, to help him sell oil and tell him what the Russians were doing. He used different strategies in different areas. Europeans, for example, wanted to buy kerosene only in small quantities, so Rockefeller supplied tank wagons to sell them oil street by street. As Allan Nevins notes:

> The [foreign] stations were kept in the same beautiful order as in the United States. Everywhere the steel storage tanks, as in America, were protected from fire by proper spacing and excellent fire-fighting ap-

> paratus. Everywhere the familiar blue barrels were of the best quality. Everywhere a meticulous neatness was evident. Pumps, buckets, and tools were all clean and under constant inspection, no litter being tolerated. . . . The oil itself was of the best quality. Nothing was left undone, in accordance with Rockefeller's long-standing policy, to make the Standard products and Standard ministrations, abroad as at home, attractive to the customer.[24]

Rockefeller's focus on quality meant that, in an evenly balanced price war with Russia, Standard Oil would win.

The Russian-American oil war was hotly contested for almost thirty years after 1885. In most markets, Standard's known reliability would prevail, if it could just get its price close to that of the Russians. In some years this meant that Rockefeller had to sell oil for 5.2 cents a gallon—leaving almost no profit margin—if he hoped to win the world. This he did; and Standard often captured two-thirds of the world's oil trade from 1882 to 1891 and a somewhat smaller portion in the decade after this.

Rockefeller and his partners always knew that their victory was a narrow triumph of efficiency over superior natural advantages. "If," as John Archbold said in 1899, "there had been as prompt and energetic action on the part of the Russian oil industry as was taken by the Standard Oil Company, the Russians would have dominated many of the world markets. . . ."[25]

At one level, Standard's ability to sell oil at close to a nickel a gallon meant hundreds of thousands of jobs for Americans in general and Standard Oil in particular. Rockefeller's margin of victory in this competition was always narrow. Even a rise of one cent a gallon would have cost Rockefeller much of his foreign market. A rise of three cents a gallon would have cost Rockefeller his American markets as well.

At another level, oil at almost a nickel a gallon opened new possibilities for people around the world. William H. Libby, Standard's foreign agent, saw this change and marveled at it. To the governor general of India he said:

> I may claim for petroleum that it is something of a civilizer, as promoting among the poorest classes of these countries a host of evening occupations, industrial, educational, and recreative, not feasible prior to its introduction; and if it has brought a fair reward to the capital ventured in its development, it has also carried more cheap comfort into more poor homes than almost any discovery of modern times.[26]

In Standard Oil, Rockefeller arguably built the most successful business in American history. In running it, he showed the precision of a bookkeeper and the imagination of an entrepreneur. Yet, in day-to-day operations, he led quietly and inspired loyalty by example. Rockefeller displayed none of the tantrums of a Vanderbilt or a Hill, and none of the flamboyance of a Schwab. At board meetings, he would sit and patiently listen to all arguments. Until the end, he would often say nothing. But his fellow directors all testified to his genius for sorting out the relevant details and pushing the right decision, even when it was shockingly bold and unpopular. "You ask me what makes Rockefeller the unquestioned leader in our group," said John Archbold, later a president of Standard Oil. "Well, it is simple. In business we all try to look ahead as far as possible. Some of us think we are pretty able. But Rockefeller always sees a little further ahead than any of us—and then he sees around the corner!"[27]

Some of these peeks around the corner helped Rockefeller pick the right people for the right jobs. He had to delegate a great deal of responsibility, and he always gave credit—and sometimes large bonuses—for work well done. Paying higher than market wages was Rockefeller's controversial policy: he believed it helped slash costs in the long run. For example, Standard was rarely hurt by strikes or labor unrest. Also, he could recruit and keep the top talent and command their future loyalty. Rockefeller approached the ideal of the "Standard Oil family" and tried to get each member to work for the good of the whole. As Thomas Wheeler said, "He managed somehow to get everybody interested in saving, in cutting out a detail here and there. . . ." He sometimes joined the men in their work, and urged them on. At 6:30 in the morning there was Rockefeller "rolling barrels, piling hoops, or wheeling out shavings." In the oil fields, there was Rockefeller trying to fit nine barrels on a eight-barrel wagon. He came to know the oil business inside out and won the respect of his workers. Praise he would give; rebukes he would avoid. "Very well kept—very indeed," said Rockefeller to an accountant about his books before pointing out a minor error and leaving. One time a new accountant moved into a room where Rockefeller kept an exercise machine. Not knowing what Rockefeller looked like, the accountant saw him and ordered him to remove it. "All right," said Rockefeller, and he politely took it away. Later, when the embarrassed accountant found out whom he had chided, he expected to be fired; but Rockefeller never mentioned it.[28]

Rockefeller treated his top managers as conquering heroes and gave them praise, rest, and comfort. He knew that good ideas were almost priceless: they were the foundation for the future of Standard Oil. To one of his oil buyers, Rockefeller wrote, "I trust you will not worry about the business. Your health is more important to you and to us than the business." Long vacations at full pay were Rockfeller's antidotes for his weary leaders. After Johnson N. Camden consolidated the West Virginia and Maryland refineries for Standard Oil, Rockefeller said, "Please feel at perfect liberty to break away three, six, nine, twelve, fifteen months, more or less. . . . Your salary will not cease, however long you decide to remain away from business." But neither Camden nor the others rested long. They were too anxious to succeed in what they were doing and to please the leader who trusted them so. Thomas Wheeler, an oil buyer for Rockefeller, said, "I have never heard of his equal in getting together a lot of the very best men in one team and inspiring each man to do his best for the enterprise."[29]

Not just Rockefeller's managers, his fellow entrepreneurs thought he was remarkable. In 1873, the prescient Commodore Vanderbilt said, "That Rockefeller! He will be the richest man in the country." Twenty years later, Charles Schwab learned of Rockefeller's versatility when Rockefeller invested almost $40 million in the controversial ore of the Mesabi iron range near the Great Lakes. Schwab said, "Our experts in the Carnegie Company did not believe in the Mesabi ore fields. They thought the ore was poor. . . . They ridiculed Rockefeller's investments in the Mesabi." But by 1901, Carnegie, Schwab, and J. P. Morgan had changed their minds and offered Rockefeller almost $90 million for his ore investments.[30]

That Rockefeller was a genius is widely admitted. What is puzzling is his philosophy of life. He was a practicing Christian and believed in doing what the Bible said to do. Therefore, he organized his life in the following way: he put God first, his family second, and career third. This is the puzzle: how could someone put his career third and wind up with $900 million, which made him the wealthiest man in American history? This is not something that can be easily explained (at least not by conventional historical methods), but it can be studied.

Rockefeller always said the best things he had done in life were to make Jesus his savior and to make Laura Spelman his wife. He prayed daily the first thing in the morning and went to church for prayer meetings with his family at least twice a week. He often said he felt most at home in church and in regular need of "spiritual food"; he and his wife also taught Bible classes and had ministers and evangelists regularly in their home.[31]

Going to church, of course, is not necessarily a sign of a practicing Christian. Ivan the Terrible regularly prayed and went to church before and after torturing and killing his fellow men. Even Commodore Vanderbilt sang hymns out of one side of his mouth and out of the other he spewed a stream of obscenities.

Rockefeller, by contrast, read the Bible and tried to practice its teachings in his everyday life. Therefore, he tithed, rested on the Sabbath, and gave valuable time to his family. This made his life hard to understand for his fellow businessmen. But it explains why he sometimes gave tens of thousands of dollars to Christian groups, while, at the same time, he was trying to borrow over a million dollars to expand his business. It explains why he rested on Sunday, even as the Russians were mobilizing to knock him out of European markets. It explains why he calmly rocked his daughter to sleep at night, even though oil prices may have dropped to an all-time low that day. Others panicked, but Rockefeller believed that God would pull him through if only he would follow His commandments. He worked to the best of his ability, then turned his problems over to God and tried not to worry. This is what he often said:

> Early I learned to work and to play.
> I dropped the worry on the way.
> God was good to me every day.[32]

Those who heard him say this may have thought that he was mouthing platitudes, but the key to understanding Rockefeller is to recognize that he said it because he believed it.

When the Russians sold their oil in Standard's blue barrels, Rockefeller did not get into strife. He knew that the book of James said, "Where strife is there is confusion and every evil work." He fought the Russians, using his spies and his authority to stop them and outsell them; but he never slandered them or threatened them. No matter what, Rockefeller never lost his temper, either. This was one of the remarkable findings of Allan Nevins in his meticulous research on Rockefeller. During the 1930s, Nevins interviewed dozens of people who worked with Rockefeller and knew him intimately.

Not one—son, daughter, friend, or foe—could ever recall Rockefeller losing his temper or even being perturbed. He was always calm.[33]

The most famous example is the time Judge K. M. Landis fined Standard Oil of Indiana over $29 million. The charge was taking rebates; and Landis, an advocate of government intervention, publicly read the verdict of "guilty" for Standard Oil. *Railway World* was shocked that "Standard Oil Company of Indiana was fined an amount equal to seven or eight times the value of its entire property, because its traffic department did not verify the statement of the Alton rate clerk that the six-cent commodity rate on oil had been properly filed with the Interstate Commerce Commission." The *New York Times* called this decision a bad law and "a manifestation of that spirit of vindictive savagery toward corporations. . . ." But Rockefeller, who had testified at the trial, was unruffled.

On the day of the verdict, he chose to play golf with friends. In the middle of their game, a frantic messenger came running through the fairways to deliver the bad news to Rockefeller. He calmly looked at the telegram, put it away, and said, "Well, shall we go on, gentlemen?" Then he hit his ball a convincing 160 yards. At the next hole, someone sheepishly asked Rockefeller, "How much is it?" Rockefeller said, "Twenty-nine million two hundred forty thousand dollars," and added, "the maximum penalty, I believe. Will you gentlemen drive?" He ended the nine holes with a respectable score of 53, as though he hadn't a care in the world.[34]

Landis' decision was eventually overruled, but Rockefeller was not so lucky in his fight against the Sherman Anti-trust Act. Rockefeller had set up a trust system at Standard Oil merely to allow his many oil businesses in different states to be headed by the same board of directors. Some states, like Pennsylvania, had laws permitting it to tax all of the property of any corporation located within state borders. Under these conditions, Rockefeller found it convenient to establish separate Standard Oil corporations in many different states, but have them directed in harmony, or in trust, by the same group of men. The Supreme Court struck this system down in 1911 and forced Standard Oil to break up into separate state companies with separate boards of directors.

This decision was puzzling to Rockefeller and his supporters. The Sherman Act was supposed to prevent monopolies and those companies "in restraint of trade." Yet Standard Oil had no monopoly and certainly was not restraining trade. The Russians, with the help of their government, had been gaining ground on Standard in the international oil trade. In America, competition in the oil industry was more intense than ever. Over one hundred oil companies—from Gulf Oil in Texas to Associated Oil in California—competed with Standard. Standard's share of the United States and world markets had been steadily declining from 1900 to 1910. Rockefeller, however, took the decision calmly and promised to obey it.[35]

Even more remarkable than Rockefeller's serenity was his diligence in tithing. From the time of his first job, where he earned 50 cents a day, the sixteen-year-old Rockefeller gave to his local Baptist church, to missions in New York City and abroad, and to the poor—black or white. As his salary increased, so did his giving. By the time he was 45, he was up to $100,000 per year; at age 53, he topped the $1,000,000 mark in his annual giving. His eightieth year was his most generous: $138,000,000 he happily gave away.[36]

The more he earned the more he gave, and the more he gave the more he earned. To Rockefeller, it was the true fulfillment of the Biblical law: "Give, and it shall be given unto you; good measure, pressed down, and shaken together, and running over, shall men give unto your bosom." Not "money" itself but "the love of money" was "the root of all evil." And Rockefeller loved God much more than his money. He learned what the prophet Malachi meant when he said, "Bring the whole tithe into the storehouse, . . . and see if I will not throw open the floodgates of heaven and pour out so much blessing that you will not have room enough for it." He learned what Jesus meant when he said, "With the measure you use, it will be measured to you." So when Rockefeller proclaimed: "God gave me [my] money," he did so in humility and in awe of the way he believed God worked.[37]

Some historians haven't liked the way Rockefeller made his money, but few have quibbled with the way he spent it. Before he died, he had given away about $550,000,000, more than any other American before him had ever possessed. It wasn't so much the amount that he gave as it was the amazing results that his giving produced. At one level he built schools and churches and supported evangelists and missionaries all over the world. After all, Jesus said, "Go ye into all the world, and preach the gospel to every creature."

Healing the sick and feeding the poor were also part of Rockefeller's Christian mission. Not state aid, but Rockefeller philanthropy paid teams of scientists who found cures for yellow fever, meningitis,

The Bettmann Archive

Rockefeller (1839–1937): Before he died, he had given away about $550,000,000 to charity, more than any other American before him had ever possessed.

and hookworm. The boll weevil was also a Rockefeller target, and the aid he gave in fighting it improved farming throughout the South.

Rockefeller attacked social and medical problems the same way he attacked the Russians—with efficiency and innovation. To get both of these, Rockefeller gave scores of millions of dollars to higher education. The University of Chicago alone got over $35,000,000. Black schools, Southern schools, and Baptist schools also reaped what Rockefeller had sown. His guide for giving was a variation of the Biblical principle—"If any would not work, neither should he eat." Those schools, cities, or scientists who weren't anxious to produce or improve didn't get Rockefeller money. Those who did and showed results got more. As in the parable of the talents, to him who has, more (responsibility and trust) shall be given by the Rockefeller Foundation.[38]

At about age sixty, Rockefeller began to wind down his remarkable business career to focus more on philanthropy, his family, and leisure. He took up gardening, started riding more on his horses, and began playing golf. Yale University might ban the tango, but Rockefeller hired an instructor to teach him how to do it. Even in recreation, Rockefeller wanted to discipline his actions for the best result. In golf, he hired a caddy to say, "Hold your head down," before each of his swings. He even strapped his left foot down with croquet wickets to keep it steady during his drives. [39]

In a way, Rockefeller's life was a paradox. He was fascinated with human nature and enjoyed studying people. Yet his unparalleled success in business made friendships awkward and forced him to shut out much of the world. To his children Rockefeller was the man who played blind man's bluff with great gusto, balanced dinner plates on his nose, and taught them how to swim and to ride bicycles. But from the world he had to keep his distance: he was a target for fortune hunters, fawners, chiselers, mountebank preachers, and hundreds of hard-luck letters written to him each week.[40]

Retirement, however, liberated him more to enjoy people and nature. On his estate in New York, he studied plants and flowers. Sometimes he would drive out into the countryside just to admire a wheatfield. Down in Florida, he liked to watch all the people who passed his house and guess at what they did in life. He handed out dimes to the neighborhood children and urged them to work and to save.[41]

Naturally, Rockefeller had some disappointments in his last years. He was sad that Standard Oil had been broken up by the Sherman Act and that the Russians had increased their foreign oil sales. He was also saddened by the Great Depression of the 1930s. Still, Rockefeller knew he had lived a full life and had been a key part of the two big transformations in the oil industry: the making of kerosene for lighting homes and the making of gasoline for running cars. Rockefeller loved life and wanted to live to be one-hundred, but he died in his sleep during his ninety-eighth year in 1937.

"Cutting Taxes to Raise Revenue"

Andrew Mellon, 1921

CHAPTER SIX

Andrew Mellon and the 1920s

Andrew Mellon is one of the most misunderstood men in American history. As Secretary of Treasury, he persuaded Congress to cut taxes to help generate the capital that made the 1920s so prosperous for so many Americans. But many textbooks claim he aided only the rich, and that he helped trigger the Great Depression. Even during the 1920s, when Mellon became one of the best known men in America, he stirred emotions with his sensational tax plan. If we look at the facts, and cut away the myth, the story of Andrew Mellon can tell us much about which tax policies work and which don't.

We all think we know that raising taxes increases revenue and that slashing taxes always lowers revenue. But Mellon challenged this conventional wisdom. "It seems difficult for some to understand," he wrote, "that high rates of taxation do not necessarily mean large revenue to the Government, and that more revenue may often be obtained by lower rates."[1] Had Mellon not been a success as an oil and aluminum entrepreneur, few would have taken his tax philosophy seriously. Yet on December 14, 1929, the U. S. Senate passed Mellon's sixth and final tax cut of the decade. It climaxed his tax revolution: from 1921 to 1929 the tax rates on those earning under $4000 per year had been chopped eightfold (from 4 to ½ percent); those in the $4000 to $8000 bracket had their burden slashed fourfold (from 8 to 2 percent); and taxes on top incomes had been cut threefold (from 73 to 24 percent). And the result for Mellon in government revenue was a startling triumph: the personal income-tax receipts for 1929 were over $1 billion, in contrast to the $719 million raised in 1921, when tax rates were so much higher. Editors, economists, and politicians across the nation were astonished and many labeled Mellon "the greatest Secretary of Treasury since Alexander Hamilton."[2]

I

Andrew Mellon came by his philosophy of low taxes and limited government quite naturally. His grandfather, a thrifty Scots-Irishman, fled Ulster in 1818 to escape the high taxes of the Napoleonic Wars. He farmed near Pittsburgh and taught his son Thomas, Andrew's father, to avoid debt, be honest, and work hard in life. As Thomas later wrote, "the hardships experienced by. . . my own parents, from oppressive taxation, became so thoroughly ingrained in my nature, when a child, that I have always felt a strong opposition . . . to all measures rendering an increase of taxes necessary. It was the universal complaint which drove our people from their homes. . . ."[3]

Young Thomas became more than a tax critic. He moved to Pittsburgh to practice law, start a bank, and raise a family. He developed a knack for finance and trained his five sons at the dinner table in how to use money to make money. Andrew, born in 1855, proved to be an eager learner. At age nine, he learned about supply and demand by selling apples from the family orchard. As a teenager Andrew went on business trips for his father, buying land near Baltimore and hiring a theater operator in Philadelphia. He went into the lumber business with his brother Richard and sold out at a nice profit just before the Panic of 1873. Thomas, a proud father, retired early and turned the family bank over to Andrew and Richard, his two youngest sons.[4]

They were an excellent team: Richard was outgoing and jovial; Andrew was introverted and quiet. Richard would greet customers and do ribbon cuttings; Andrew would do more of the thinking and planning. Many workers at T. Mellon and Sons Bank, even some officers, knew Richard as a friend but knew Andrew hardly at all, even by sight. Andrew was 5'9" tall, lean in body, sharp in features, and had a thick moustache. For exercise he liked to walk and did so with a firm pace and erect back, even into his seventies. When he spoke, which was not often, his voice was soft, like a whisper. He would sometimes preface his words with a slight cough. Pauses were frequent. Yet his mouselike manner hid a mental toughness that always commanded respect. When Andrew gave advice, ears strained to listen.[5]

What Mellon lacked in rhetorical skill he made up for with his exceptional judgment of people and ideas. He had a remarkably creative mind and liked to think about strategies that would change industry and society. As a banker, for example, he backed industrialists who were strong on ideas but weak on finances. The production of aluminum, for example, was slow, expensive, and irrelevant to most Americans in the 1890s. But when Mellon backed Alcoa he believed that aluminum, with its light weight and excellent conducting qualities, would challenge steel and copper as a major industrial metal. Mellon and his family sank $15 million into Gulf Oil in the early 1900s, because he believed that they could build and run a vertically-integrated oil company that could compete with mighty Standard Oil. He was right; Gulf built pipelines from Texas to Oklahoma, invented offshore drilling, and built the first corner service stations to provide gas for cars.[6]

The key to the success of these industries, and dozens of other Mellon enterprises, was capital—high-risk, venture capital. Somebody had to have the nerve, the money, and the vision to back risky ideas that had potential. Mellon had done this so ably that by 1920 he was worth close to one billion dollars, which ranked him with John D. Rockefeller and Henry Ford as one of the three wealthiest men in America. Mellon's superior grasp of economics caught the attention of national political leaders after World War I. They were struggling with a stagnant economy, a rising national debt, and a crushing tax burden. Republican Warren G. Harding, winner of the 1920 Presidential election, asked Mellon to be his Secretary of Treasury and do for the American economy what he had done with aluminum and oil.[7]

Mellon hesitated to accept Harding's offer. In the industrial world he directed a worldwide economic empire. He would have to resign his position on the boards of directors of sixty corporations to take a $12,000-a-year job trying to straighten out a mess. At age 65, though, Mellon had been the entrepreneur long enough. His family urged him to accept, and he was challenged by the idea of applying his business experience to government problems. So Mellon went to Washington, bought an apartment on Massachusetts Avenue, and took command of the Treasury Department. In a sense, he was very comfortable with his work: corporate problems and government problems were often similar; he delegated the detail work to his undersecretaries and applied his talent to strengthening the postwar economy. In another sense, Mellon had to make adjustments. Newspapers publicized his wealth and reporters pried into his life. They freely accosted him, even as he walked to work. The taciturn Mellon stumbled so completely in his first interview that he couldn't articulate a thought. After some practice, and some good press clippings, Mellon warmed up to most reporters. All through his term, though, the less he was forced to say about something the more at ease he was. When Mellon held a press conference, or spoke before Congress, he usually wrote out his message and had his undersecretary read it. If possible, he even had the undersecretary field the questions.[8]

Mellon came to Washington at a crucial time in U. S. history. World War I had been a turning point in the way many perceived the role of government in economic life. Before the war, the federal role in operating, regulating, and taxing American business was small. Federal budgets were less than $1 billion per year. The taxes needed to run the American government were low and fairly easily collected; land sales and tariffs were the major sources of revenue.[9] In the 1910s, two things helped change all of this: the passing of the income tax and the outbreak of the First World War.

The idea of taxing incomes had long been debated in American history. During the Civil War, Congress passed a 3 percent tax on all incomes over $800, and raised the rate and taxable amounts twice, but repealed the tax in 1872. Then in 1894, during an economic downturn, Congress passed a flat 2 percent tax on all incomes over $4000. The next year, however, the Supreme Court declared this law unconstitutional. Conservatives tended to oppose the income tax: high taxes stifled investment, they argued, and any income tax, once passed, was easy to raise and hard to reduce. Existing taxes were adequate, conservatives argued, and business should be left relatively free. "Progressives," as they called themselves, favored the income tax and fought to pass a constitutional amendment giving Congress the right to levy taxes on personal and corporate incomes. The income tax, in Progressive theory, could be used instead of tariffs to raise revenue, and also to increase the powers of the federal government. The leading Progressive spokesmen during the 1920s were Senators Robert M. LaFollette of Wisconsin, George W. Norris of Nebraska, and James Couzens of Michigan.[10]

The period from 1900 to 1920 is sometimes called the Progressive Era because during this time Progressives entered politics and increased the role of the federal government in the American economy. In 1913, they secured the 16th amendment, which enabled Congress to tax personal incomes. The income tax passed that year was light: individuals earning less than $3000 per year and married couples making $4000 per year paid no tax. Those who earned more were taxed only 1 percent up to $20,000 income. Then the tax became progressive, that is, the rates increased as income increased. Those earning from $20,000 to $50,000 were taxed at 2 percent; from $50,000 to $75,000 at 3 percent; and so on. The top rate was 7 percent of incomes over $500,000. Under this law, few Americans paid any income taxes; of those who did, most paid only 1 percent. The revenue raised from this law was small, but the government itself was small in 1913 and it needed little revenue to run efficiently.[11]

In 1916, in response to President Wilson's program of preparedness for war, Congress hiked the income tax rate. It became 2 percent on incomes under $20,000 and rose to 15 percent on incomes of $2 million or more. The exemptions were unchanged. The next year the U. S. entered the First World War: expenses soared to the highest levels in U. S. history; massive government programs bought food, weapons, and equipment for America and her allies. The government also set prices and wages, and controlled production of scores of industries. Wilson used the income tax to raise much of the money needed to wage war: rates started at 4 percent and soared to 77 percent on top incomes. Corporate taxes rose to 18 percent. Most Americans were willing to sacrifice for this emergency and paid over $7 billion in taxes during the war years. They also bought billions of dollars in "Liberty bonds" to aid the allied cause. In the wake of military victory, the national debt had skyrocketed from $1.5 billion in 1916 to $24 billion in 1919.[12]

This controlled economy fulfilled the dream of many Progressives. They had problems, though, when the revenue raised from high taxes plunged in 1919 and 1920. The federal spending that Progressives desired could not continue after the war because of this shrinking revenue and a dramatic increase in the national debt. "There is a point," President Wilson discovered, "at which in peace times high rates of income and profits taxes discourage energy . . . and produce industrial stagnation with consequent unemployment and other . . . evils." The by-products of war—high taxes and a soaring national debt—would clearly be issues in the 1920s. Andrew Mellon agreed with Wilson's new way of thinking and went from there.[13]

As Treasury Secretary, Mellon carefully collected and studied data on the American economy. High taxes, he concluded, were the chief parasites draining the lifeblood of the American economy. "Before the period of the war," he observed, "taxes as high as those now in effect would have been thought fantastic and impossible of payment." Rich men went to great lengths to avoid paying the 73 percent rate Mellon confronted when he came to Washington.

> The high rates inevitably put pressure upon the taxpayer to withdraw his capital from productive business and invest it in tax-exempt securities. . . .The result is that the sources of taxation are drying up; wealth is failing to carry its share of the tax burden; and capital is being diverted into channels which yield neither revenue to the Government nor profit to the people.[14]

Mellon publicized the evidence in Table 1 to make his point. Between 1916 and 1921, the number of people who earned over $300,000 per year had shrunk, and so had their average incomes. The rich were not poorer but wiser; they were shifting their fortunes into tax-exempt bonds.

The subject of tax-exempt bonds became relevant because Congress allowed cities and states to issue bonds that were free of any taxes. When tax rates were higher than 50 percent on top incomes, municipal bonds that paid about 5 percent were more attractive to wealthy people than taxable investments that paid 11 percent. Since almost no corporation in the country consistently

Table 1: The Decline of Taxable Incomes Over $300,000 From 1916 to 1921

Year	Number of Returns		Net Income	
	All classes	Incomes over $300,000	All classes	Incomes over $300,000
1916 . .	437,036	1,296	$ 6,298,577,620	$992,972,986
1917 . .	3,472,890	1,015	13,652,383,207	731,372,153
1918 . .	4,425,114	627	15,924,639,355	401,107,868
1919 . .	5,332,760	679	19,859,491,448	440,011,589
1920 . .	7,259,944	395	23,735,629,183	246,354,585
1921 . .	6,662,176	246	19,577,212,528	153,534,305

Source: Andrew Mellon, *Taxation: The People's Business* (New York: Macmillan, 1924), 74.

earned 11 percent per year, capital flooded into bonds for projects in cities all over the country.[15]

Mellon estimated in 1923 that Americans held fully $12 billion—a threefold increase in ten years—in tax-exempt bonds. This $12 billion was almost three times the amount of the federal budget and more than half of the debt owed by the national government. All of these rich people pouring cash into municipal bonds alarmed Mellon: America's industries, he argued, were starving for capital while the cities had abundant low-interest cash available whether they needed it or not. Thus, the U. S. had more and more large football stadiums and civic centers but fewer and fewer factories where these cityfolks could work long-term jobs.[16]

Mellon knew firsthand how hard it was for speculative ventures—such as making aluminum or drilling for oil—to raise the money needed for success. Poor or middle-class people, living from payday to payday, could rarely afford to invest in these high-risk ventures. Only the wealthy could afford the risk and supply the capital to start up high-risk industries. When the top incomes in the U. S. shifted away from corporate development and into tax-exempt bonds, new industries especially had trouble raising the capital to compete. But, Mellon insisted, the whole economy suffered, too. He used William Rockefeller, the brother of John D., as an example of high taxes chasing capital out of productive investment. When Rockefeller died in 1923, Mellon discovered that he had $44 million in tax-exempt bonds and only $7 million left in Standard Oil.[17] Mellon urged Congress to support a law—even a constitutional amendment—to abolish the tax-free status of city and state bonds. But he knew this was no quick fix. As long as taxes were high, investors would find some way to avoid them. Taxes had to be slashed "to attract the large fortunes back into productive enterprise." Then Mellon added a twist to his argument: "more revenue [for the government], may often be obtained by lower rates." Not just more revenue from the rich, Mellon predicted, but more revenue overall might come to the government if taxes were cut. He compared the government setting tax rates on incomes to a businessman setting prices on products. "If a price is fixed too high, sales drop off and with them profits." Mellon asked:

> Does anyone question that Mr. Ford has made more money by reducing the price of his car [from $3000 to $380] and increasing his sales than

> he would have made by maintaining a high price and a greater profit per car, but selling less [sic] cars?

Mellon, of course, recognized that there was a limit to how far you could cut taxes and still increase revenue. "The problem of the government," he said, "is to fix rates which will bring in a maximum amount of revenue to the Treasury and at the same time bear not too heavily on the taxpayer or on business enterprises." Mellon believed that 25 percent was about as much as rich people would pay in taxes before they rushed to the tax shelters.[18]

Mellon's prediction that lowering tax rates might produce more revenue for the government was controversial right from the start. Progressives shuddered at the thought; but even conservatives were nervous. At stake to conservatives was balancing the budget and shrinking the high national debt. Over $7.5 billion worth of 4 percent Liberty bonds was coming due in 1923. None of the bonds could be paid off if Mellon was wrong. The government would have to renegotiate these bonds, probably at higher rates, and then borrow more each year to make up for lower revenues and for the added interest payments on the national debt. It would then be harder in the future to balance the budget, confidence in the American government would fall, interest rates might rise, and investors might withdraw capital from the American economy. The economic downturn after the war might persist through the 1920s. Mellon quietly waged his war of ideas first with Harding and then with Coolidge till both decided to back him.[19]

Mellon was an odd sort of man to command such attention in the Harding-Coolidge administration. After Harding was elected, he invited Mellon to come to his home in Marion, Ohio, to discuss the Treasury job. Mellon took the train to Marion and found no one in the depot to meet him. So he walked the mile to Harding's house, suitcase in hand, and waited in line—behind local job-seekers—to have his appointment with Harding. When the astounded clerk realized Mellon was waiting in the reception room, Mellon refused to have any fuss made and insisted on taking his turn behind the others. When Mellon's turn finally came, he spent much of the time trying to talk Harding out of choosing him to head the Treasury Department. At last, Harding had a man for his cabinet who was not seeking glory and who couldn't be bought.[20]

Sometimes Mellon's humility created embarrassments. At a press banquet Mellon was mistakenly called to the phone and ended up being asked to take a long message for some reporter named George. Mellon dutifully took three pages of notes from the stranger and delivered them to George.[21]

In Harding's administration, Mellon's low-key personality and his encyclopedic knowledge of economics became legendary. At a cabinet meeting in 1921, the question came up whether the U. S. should scrap a war factory that had cost $12 million, or a similar amount should be spent to refurbish it. Finally, Mellon was asked his opinion.

> Mr. Mellon was hesitant. Then he spoke up in his low, quiet, dry voice. The matter was not exactly in his department; he had not given the problem any study; he was not familiar with all the conditions and the full situation; it was a question of some importance; he did not wish to be understood as giving his final opinion unless he had opportunity to go into the whole matter more fully, but he thought he could indicate possibly what his final judgment might be, if allowed to tell what he had done in a somewhat similar and personal case. He owned a war plant that stood him about fifteen or sixteen millions, and just the other day the question had come up whether to spend that much more money on it or to wipe it off. "I told 'em to scrap it," concluded Mr. Mellon.[22]

And so the government scrapped its war plant. In a later cabinet meeting on international relations, the subject of the Chinese Eastern Railway came up:

> The President leaned over to Attorney General [Harry] Daugherty and whispered, "Now we've got him. Surely he wasn't in this."
>
> "I don't suppose, Mellon," said President Harding, winking at Daugherty, and assuming a most casual manner, "that you were interested in the Chinese Eastern Railway, were you?"
>
> "Oh, yes," Mr. Mellon replied placidly; "we had a million or a million and a half of the bonds." And he told the cabinet all about the road; all about it—not part—all.
>
> "It's no use," said the President, "no use. He's the ubiquitous financier of the universe."[23]

As the resident "financier of the universe," Mellon commanded respect; and in 1924 when he wrote *Taxation: The People's Business*, he had full presidential support. The press dubbed his proposal the "Mellon Plan." Its four main points were:

1. *Cut the top income tax rate to 25 percent*. This was one of the first things Mellon had tried to do when he took office. In 1921 Congress did cut the top rate from 73 to 58 percent; but after this the resistance stiffened. The Progressives wanted a high tax rate on the rich and they had the logic of democratic politics on their side: few voters earned large incomes; many voters resented those who did, and therefore there was always support for a soak-the-rich policy. Mellon believed that about 25 percent was the most that investors would pay before they fled to tax-exempt bonds. Cutting the top tax to 25 percent would, he predicted, bring the large fortunes back into productive enterprise and might generate a surplus of revenue for the government.[24]

2. *Cut taxes on low incomes*. When Mellon took office the existing rates were 4 percent on those incomes of $4000 or less, and 8 percent on incomes over $4000. Mellon wanted to cut these rates from 4 to 3 percent and from 8 to 6 percent; later he argued that these rates should be cut even further. No doubt Mellon was being politically shrewd with this part of his plan, but he also seems to have believed in what he was doing. Tax policy, he argued, "must lessen, so far as possible, the burden of taxation on those least able to bear it." To further this end, he also suggested an income-tax credit of 25 percent on earned income—that is, income earned by wages would be taxed less than income earned through investments. Mellon also proposed a repeal of the federal taxes on telegrams, telephones, and movie tickets. The tax on movie tickets, especially, was a fee "paid by the great bulk of the people whose main source of recreation is attending the movies in the neighborhood of their homes. The loss in revenue would be about seventy million dollars, but it would constitute a direct saving to a large number of people whose tax burden should be lightened wherever it is possible to do so."[25]

But Progressives often opposed cutting the tax rates even on the lower-income groups. When the income tax first became law, for example, Robert LaFollette wanted the taxing to start at $10,000, instead of $20,000. In later Congressional debates he often tried to reduce the personal exemptions, so that taxes would start on incomes of $1,000, instead of $2,000. As Governor of Wisconsin, he pushed for a bill that allowed the state to start taxing those who made as little as $800. When LaFollette died in 1925, his son, Robert Jr., went to the Senate and picked up where his father left off. He joined thirteen other Progressive senators in voting against

Mellon's bill to cut taxes from 1½ to ½ percent on those earning less than $4,000 per year.[26]

3. *Reduce the federal estate tax.* In 1916 Congress passed the first federal inheritance tax. The rates were progressive and started on estates of over $50,000. By the time Mellon took office the top rate had been increased from 5 to 25 percent. Progressives pushed the maximum up to 40 percent at the same time the Mellon Plan was launched. Mellon opposed this vigorously. He thought that states, not the federal government, should enjoy the revenue from inheritance taxes. He also argued that stocks and properties in large estates could not net their full value because with high taxes they would have to be sold quickly by heirs. Furthermore, large estate taxes, like large income taxes, tempted the wealthy to shift their fortunes into tax-exempt shelters.[27] In the case of large estates, the shelter would be tax-exempt foundations, as Mellon would show in the 1930s.

4. *Efficiency in government.* The 1919 federal budget was over $18 billion; Mellon wanted to see annual budgets drop below $4 billion. Smaller budgets meant less need for tax revenues and also greater ease in reducing the $24 billion national debt. In the Treasury Department Mellon cut personal expenses; he also cut from the Treasury Department staff an average of one person per day every day during the 1920s. He was able to do this because lower tax rates meant fewer returns, which meant fewer people were needed to process and audit returns. Mellon had other ideas, too. He cut the size of paper bills to fit wallets more easily and thereby saved expenses on paper and ink.[28]

The Mellon Plan was probably the subject of more debate than any other political issue during the 1920s. Not just the money was involved; two political ideologies were clashing. In a sense, it made little difference whether a man making $4000 paid $120 tax under the old rates, or $67.50 under the Mellon Plan. But the Progressives wanted to take these small amounts, add them to the huge windfalls they hoped to extract from the rich, and use the money to back the McNary-Haugen bill, which authorized the government to help farmers market their surplus crops; pay a cash bonus to veterans of World War I; and pay for the federal development of hydroelectric power along the Tennessee River Valley. Mellon, by contrast, wanted to use any surplus revenue from tax cutting to retire the national debt. He called the Progressive agenda "taking money out of the pockets of all the people in order that it shall find its way back into the pockets of some of the people."[29]

Mellon made one exception to his theme of limited government—he favored a tariff. Perhaps he felt obligated to support a tariff because the Republican party endorsed one. Still, it created inconsistencies in his argument and opened him to attack. When the Republicans passed the Fordney-McCumber Tariff in 1922, Mellon seemed comfortable supporting it. Included in this tariff was a three-cent-a pound rise in the duty on imported aluminum. Mellon, of course, had divested himself of his Alcoa interests when he went to Washington, but there was still understandable criticism of him. Senator William Borah, a Progressive from Idaho, attacked Mellon for opposing government protection for farmers but favoring government protection for Alcoa.[30]

The debate between Mellon and the Progressives was fought almost every year in Congress. In the early 1920s, the sides were about evenly matched. In the tax bills of 1921, 1922, and 1924, Mellon and his supporters reduced the rates on large personal incomes to 46 percent, a minor victory; corporation taxes, however, were raised from 10 to 12.5 percent, a minor defeat. Progressives had the rates on large estates hiked from 25 to 40 percent. They also enacted a gift tax to prevent the rich from giving their fortunes away before they died. Mellon did get his lower rates on incomes below $8,000, but this was less controversial because it was so politically popular. The Democratic party leaders also suggested lower rates and, on occasion, so did Progressives.[31]

When Harding died in 1923 and Coolidge became President, Mellon found himself with a strong ally to help break the Congressional deadlock. Coolidge studied the tax problem and agreed with Mellon's conclusions. "I agree perfectly," Coolidge said, "with those who wish to relieve the small taxpayer by getting the largest possible contribution from the people with large incomes. But if the rates on large incomes are so high that they disappear, the small taxpayer will be left to bear the entire burden."[32]

Coolidge and Mellon not only thought alike, they acted alike. Both men were shy and at state dinners they must have made guests uneasy because they said almost nothing. Cleveland Amory wrote that Mellon and Coolidge seemed to have conversed "almost entirely in pauses." They even installed a direct phone hookup to each other, perhaps to share silence together.[33]

The two men were quiet for different reasons. Coolidge grew up on a farm in Vermont. His mother died when he was young and he saw few people as a boy, so he never developed social skills. Mellon, by contrast, had a weak speaking voice, and the presence of a crowd made him uneasy. Coolidge's political success and Mellon's business success only reinforced the problem; crowds, jobseekers, and fawners all sought these men out for favors. A retreat to silence was their response to these pressures.[34]

Both men took almost childish delight in their families. Coolidge adored his wife and bought her fancy clothes and presents. When driving his car, Coolidge allowed only family members to ride with him. Mellon, although divorced, was close to his two children, Ailsa and Paul. "With his children this quiet, reserved man was a different being from the financier the world knew," observed Mellon's nephew William. Mellon would join his children on sled rides, he would fly kites and play ball with them, or chase them in blind man's bluff. "If the children slid down the banisters, he would slide with them," his nephew observed. "He would play hide-and-seek until they were tired of the game."[35]

Distrustful of outsiders, both Coolidge and Mellon found joy in pets or possessions. Coolidge had a pet raccoon that roamed the White House freely; he was given a parrot trained to say "What about the appropriation?"; and he raised chickens in the White House back yard. Mellon had an all-aluminum car; and he assembled one of the finest art collections in the world. This closeness in personality and philosophy may have united Coolidge and Mellon and made them more forceful in their appeals for tax cuts and balanced budgets.[36]

The 1924 elections shifted the balance of power to the conservatives. Coolidge ran for re-election and won a landslide victory over the Democrats and also LaFollette, who ran as a third-party candidate. The tax cuts were a major issue in the campaign and the Republicans now had a mandate and a strong congressional majority to put them into effect. Congress passed most of the Mellon Plan in 1926. In 1928 and 1929, Mellon recommended, and Congress passed, further tax cuts: the estate tax was halved to 20 percent, top incomes paid 24 percent, and smaller incomes had even larger proportional reductions.[37]

The Progressives denigrated his achievements whenever possible. They could hardly dispute his results; instead they challenged his motives. In 1925, Senator Norris announced, "Mr.

Mellon himself gets a larger personal reduction than the aggregate of practically all the taxpayers in the state of Nebraska." The records showed, however, that Mellon also paid more in income taxes than did all of the taxpayers of Nebraska. John Nance Garner, the Democratic leader in the House, said in 1924 that the Mellon Plan had "for its sole purpose the reduction of the larger taxpayers at the expense of the smaller taxpayer." To Senator LaFollette, the Mellon Plan meant that "wealth will not and cannot be made to bear its full share of taxation."[38]

The results of Mellon's tax cuts in 1926, however, as seen in Table 2, show that the tax burden shifted toward, not away from, the rich. In 1921 people who earned less than $10,000 per year paid almost as much in total income taxes as did those who earned over $100,000 per year. In 1926, the ratios changed: those who earned over $100,000 per year paid over ten times as much in aggregate income taxes as those who earned less than $10,000 per year. Meanwhile, the total revenue from 1921 to 1926 had increased. These trends continued with Mellon's smaller tax cuts in 1928 and 1929. In 1929, the income-tax revenue surpassed $1 billion. Those in the $100,000 bracket paid 65 percent of it; those in the under $10,000 bracket paid only 1.3 percent of the total tax.[39]

As a last resort, Progressives attacked Mellon's integrity. He manipulated tax audits, they charged, and refunded $3.5 billion during the 1920s to Republican friends and to corporations in which he had a large interest. Alcoa, for example, received a $15 million refund for supposed overpayment of taxes during the war. Refunds also went to Gulf Oil and to seventeen people who contributed $10,000 to the Republican party in 1930.[40]

These attacks suggest that Mellon used his office to ladle cash

Table 2: The Tax Revenue Collected According to Income Groupings Before and After the 1926 Tax Cuts

Net Income Grouping	Tax Revenue Collected from Income Grouping (in millions of constant 1929 dollars) 1921	1926
Less than $10,000	$155.1	$ 32.5
$10,000 to $25,000	121.8	70.3
$25,000 to $50,000	108.3	109.4
$50,000 to $100,000	111.1	136.6
Over $100,000	194.0	361.5
Total	$690.2	$710.2

Source: James Gwartney, "Tax Cuts: Who Shoulders the Burden?" *Economic Review* (March 1982).

to himself and his cronies. Mellon, however, had little to do with granting refunds; a Board of Tax Appeals ruled on these cases. This Board did award $3.5 billion in refunds to taxpayers during the 1920s, as the Progressives charged; but it also reassessed other taxpayers $5.3 billion during this same period. In other words, the Treasury department took in more revenue in reassessments than it lost in refunds. And prominent Democrats, as well as Republicans, were among the winners and losers in tax cases during the 1920s.[41]

Mellon usually avoided critics and stayed out of public arguments.[42] Reporters often quoted Mellon's critics to him to see how he would respond. "It is merely vicious piffle," Mellon once said when asked about a criticism. Another time, a Republican leader asked him what he thought of Senator Borah, a regular critic of Treasury policies. Mellon replied, "I never think of him unless somebody mentions his name." Some listeners probably thought this retort was clever; but Mellon meant it. He knew his energy was limited and he wanted to spend it working on ways to strengthen the economy. "Worry," concluded Mellon, "is the sport of men who have nothing to do and plenty of time in which to make a mess of doing it."[43]

This attitude served him well in the 1930s, the last years of his life, when the New Dealers came into power and his policies came under attack. After Coolidge's term, Mellon stayed on as Herbert Hoover's Secretary of Treasury. But the two men clashed over how to respond to the Great Depression. Mellon resigned in February, 1932, and served as Hoover's Ambassador to Great Britain until Franklin Roosevelt took office as President in 1933. Under both Hoover and Roosevelt federal income taxes were raised. By 1935, the top marginal rate had again reached almost 80 percent, and investors again manipulated their investments to avoid taxes. To make up for lost revenue, Congress passed a series of excise taxes on bank checks, movie tickets, telephone calls, gasoline, tires, cars, electricity, lubricating oils, and grape concentrates. The New Deal was funded in large part by the money raised from these taxes. Excise taxes, however, are considered regressive because they hit lower income groups proportionally more heavily than richer groups. Mellon had slashed excise taxes during the 1920s to lighten the burden on the common man. But even though Mellon's tax policies were overturned, he believed that his ideas would endure and that history would vindicate his policy of low tax rates. He retired from politics, donated his $50 million art collection to the National Gallery of Art, and died peacefully in 1937.[44]

III

College textbooks have naturally devoted space to Andrew Mellon and the 1920s. One of the most widely used texts is *The National Experience* by John M. Blum of Yale, William S. McFeely of the University of Georgia, Edmund S. Morgan of Yale, Arthur Schlesinger, Jr., of the City University of New York, Kenneth Stampp of Berkeley and C. Vann Woodward of Yale. In 1993, this text went into its eighth edition. Blum and Schlesinger, who has won a Pulitzer Prize, wrote the sections on the 1920s and 1930s, and here is what they say about Mellon:

> Foremost among Harding's advisers was Secretary of the Treasury Andrew Mellon, a reticent multimillionaire from Pittsburgh whose intricate banking and investment holdings gave him, his family, and his associates control, among many other things, of the aluminum monopoly. A man of slight build, with a cold and weary face, Mellon exuded sober luxury and contemptuous worldliness. "The Government is just a business," he believed, "and can and should be run on business principles."
>
> Great businesses, as Mellon knew, thrive on innovation and expansion. Yet the only business principle he considered relevant to government was economy. With small regard for the services that only government could furnish the nation, Mellon worked unceasingly to reduce federal expenditures. Expenses had to be cut if he was to achieve his corollary purpose: the reduction of taxes, especially taxes on the wealthy. It was better, he argued, to place the burden of taxes on lower-income groups, for taxing the rich inhibited their investments and thus retarded economic growth. A share of the tax-free profits of the rich, Mellon reassured the country, would ultimately trickle down to the middle- and lower-income groups in the form of salaries and wages. Robert LaFollette paraphrased that theory succinctly: "Wealth will not and cannot be made to bear its full share of taxation."[45]

But Mellon did not want to "place the burden of taxes on lower-income groups." On the contrary, as we have seen, he cut taxes proportionally more on the lower income groups. The rich were carrying almost the entire income-tax burden after Mellon's tax cuts. It was the tax hikes of the 1930s that shifted the burden of taxation back to the lower-income groups. But Schlesinger almost completely ignores these tax hikes. He never mentions that large incomes were taxed at 63 percent after 1932, and at 79 percent after 1934. He also never mentions the new excise taxes that became law after 1932 and were used to fund New Deal programs.

Another best-selling textbook has been *The American Nation*, by John Garraty of Columbia University. Garraty describes Mellon's ideas this way:

> Mellon carried his policies to unreasonable extremes. He proposed eliminating inheritance taxes and reducing the tax on high incomes by two-thirds, but he opposed lower rates for taxpayers earning less than $66,000 a year, apparently not realizing that economic expansion required greater mass consumption as well. Freeing the rich from "oppressive" taxation, he argued, would enable them to invest more in potentially productive enterprises, the success of which would create jobs for ordinary people. Little wonder that Mellon's admirers called him the greatest secretary of the treasury since Alexander Hamilton.
>
> Although the Republicans had large majorities in both houses of Congress, Mellon's proposals were too reactionary to win unqualified approval.[46]

Garraty's account, in content and in tone, is similar to Schlesinger's. When Garraty says Mellon "opposed lower rates for taxpayers earning less than $66,000 a year. . . ." he is wrong. Those earning under $66,000 a year, as we have seen, had the largest proportional tax cut and had most of their tax burden lifted. Also, Mellon did not propose "eliminating inheritance taxes," as Garraty claims. Mellon wanted the states, not the federal government, to receive revenue from inheritance taxes. Like Schlesinger, Garraty never mentions the specific tax rates on large incomes during the 1930s. Nor does he mention the excise taxes of the New Deal period.

Probably the best-selling college history textbook is *The American Pageant* by Thomas A. Bailey and David M. Kennedy, both of Stanford. This text is in its tenth edition and has sold over two million copies, according to its promotional literature. Bailey and Kennedy describe Mellon's ideas. Then they conclude that "Mellon's spare-the-rich policies thus shifted much of the tax burden from the wealthy to the middle-income groups."[47] This, of course, is the same error that Schlesinger and Garraty make. Mellon's tax cut produced one result; and these historians have said that the opposite occurred. Bailey and Kennedy also ignore the tax increases of the 1930s.

Other texts are similar. There seems to be almost no correct information in any college history text on the impact of Mellon's tax cuts, or on the New Deal tax hikes. Yet the tax records have been available for almost sixty years. And studies of these records by Roy and Gladys Blakey, Benjamin Rader, James Gwartney, and Thomas Silver have also been available for some time. This situation is especially perplexing because Schlesinger has written well-respected books on the 1920s and 1930s, and Garraty has written widely in economic history. Expertise in the field, in fact, does not seem to correlate with presenting accurate information. Irwin Unger, for example, is also an economic historian, and even won a Pulitzer Prize for a book on the Greenback era. Yet in his textbook, *These United States*, he writes:

> [Mellon] persuaded Congress to eliminate the wartime excess-profits tax and reduce income tax rates at the upper levels while leaving those at the bottom untouched. Between 1920 and 1929 Mellon won further victories for his drive to shift more of the tax burden from high-income earners to the middle and wage-earning classes. (48)

It's hard to know who would have been more startled by Unger's account: Mellon or the lower-income taxpayers, who saw both their income and excise taxes drastically cut during the 1920s. George Santayana once said that those who do not learn from the past are condemned to repeat it. But how can we learn what happened in the past if historians either will not teach it or do not know it? National debates over tax cuts occurred in the 1960s, 1980s, and the 1990s, but how can we debate a subject intelligently if we are misinformed about the facts?[49]

Andrew Mellon never made an investment without knowing the relevant facts; his business success demonstrated his grasp of financial situations. In similar fashion, modern politicians, businessmen, and historians would do well to learn the facts of American tax history before they try to plot its future.

CHAPTER SEVEN

Entrepreneurs vs. The Historians

> A nation must believe in three things. It must believe in the past. It must believe in the future. It must, above all, believe in the capacity of its people so to learn from the past that they can gain in judgment for the creation of the future.
>
> —Franklin D. Roosevelt

One reason for studying history is to learn from it. If we can discover what worked and what didn't work, we can use this knowledge to create a better future. Studying the rise of big business, for example, is important because it is the story of how the United States prospered and became a world power. During the years in which this took place, roughly from 1840 to 1920, we had a variety of entrepreneurs who took risks and built very successful industries. We also had a state that created a stable marketplace in which these entrepreneurs could operate. However, this same state occasionally dabbled in economic development through subsidies, tariffs, regulating trade, and even running a steel plant to make armor. When the state played this kind of role, it often failed. This is the sort of information that is useful to know when we think about planning for the future.

The problem is that many historians have been teaching the opposite lesson for years. They have been saying that entrepreneurs, not the state, created the problem. Entrepreneurs, according to these historians, were often "robber barons" who corrupted politics and made fortunes bilking the public.[1] In this view, government intervention in the economy was needed to save the public from greedy businessmen. This view, with some modifications, still dominates in college textbooks in American history.

American history textbooks always have at least one chapter on the rise of big business. Most of these works, however, portray the growth of industry in America as a grim experience, an "ordeal" as one text calls it. Much of this alleged grimness is charged to entrepreneurs.[2]

Thomas Bailey, in *The American Pageant*, is typical when he says of Vanderbilt: "Though ill-educated, ungrammatical, coarse, and ruthless, he was clear-visioned. Offering superior railway service at lower rates, he amassed a fortune of $100 million."[3] If this second sentence is true, to whom was Vanderbilt "ruthless?" Not to consumers, who received "superior service at lower rates," but to his opponents, such as Edward Collins, who were using the state to extort subsidies and impose high rates on consumers. This distinction is vital and must be stressed if we are to sort out the impact of different types of entrepreneurs.

I have systematically studied three of the best-selling college textbooks in American history: *The American Pageant*, by Thomas Bailey and David Kennedy of Stanford University; *The American Nation*, by John Garraty of Columbia University; and *The National Experience*, by John Blum of Yale University, Edmund Morgan of Yale University, William S. McFeely of the University of Georgia, Arthur Schlesinger, Jr., of the City University of New York, Kenneth Stampp of the University of California at Berkeley, and C. Vann Woodward of Yale University. These works have been written by some of the most distinguished men in the historical profession; all three books have sold hundreds of thousands of copies.[4] In all three, John D. Rockefeller receives more attention than any other entrepreneur. This is probably as it should be. His story is a crucial part of the rise of big business: he dominated his industry, he drastically cut prices, he never lobbied for a government subsidy or a tariff, and he ended up as America's first near-billionaire.

The three textbooks do credit Rockefeller with cutting costs and improving the efficiency of the oil industry, but they all see his success as fraudulent. In *The National Experience*, Woodward says that:

> Rockefeller hated free competition and believed that monopoly was the way of the future. His early method of dealing with competitors was to gain unfair advantage over them through special rates and rebates

> arranged with the railroads. With the aid of these advantages, Standard became the largest refiner of oil in the country. . . . In 1881 [Standard Oil] controlled nearly 90 percent of the country's oil refining capacity and could crush any remaining competitors at will.[5]

In *The American Nation*, John Garraty commends Rockefeller for his skill but adopts roughly the same line of reasoning as does Woodward:

> Rockefeller exploited every possible technical advance and employed fair means and foul to persuade competitors either to sell out or to join forces. . . . Rockefeller competed ruthlessly not primarily to crush other refiners but to persuade them to join with him, to share the business peaceably and rationally so that all could profit. . . . Competition almost disappeared; prices steadied; profits skyrocketed. By 1892 John D. Rockefeller was worth over $800 million.[6]

In these views the cause and effect are clear: the rebates and "unfair competition" were the main causes of Rockefeller's success; this success gave him an alleged monopoly; and the alleged monopoly created his fortune. Yet as we have seen, Rockefeller's astonishing efficiency was the main reason for his success. He didn't get the largest rebates until he had the largest business. Even then, the Vanderbilts offered the same rebates to anyone who shipped as much oil on the New York Central as Rockefeller did. In any case, the rebates went largely to cutting the price of oil for consumers, not to Rockefeller himself.

Perhaps even more misleading than the faulty stress on the rebates is the omitting of the most important feature of Rockefeller's career: his thirty-year struggle with Russia to capture the world's oil markets. Not one of the three texts even mentions this oil war with Russia.

Three facts show the importance of Rockefeller's battle with the Russians. First, about two-thirds of the oil refined in America in the late 1800s was exported. Second, Russia was closer than the U. S. to all European and Asian markets. Third, Russian oil was more centralized, more plentiful, and more viscous than American oil. If Rockefeller had not overcome Russia's natural advantages, no one else could have. America would have lost millions of dollars in exports and might have even had to import oil from Russia. The spoils of victory—jobs, technology, cheap kerosene, cheap by-products, and cheap gas to spur the auto industry—all of this might have been lost had it not been for Rockefeller's ability to sell oil profitably at six cents a gallon. The omitting of the Russo-American oil war was so striking that I checked every college American history text that I could find (twenty total) to see if this is typical. It is. Only one of the twenty textbooks even mentions the Russian oil competition.[7]

Obviously textbooks can't include everything. Nor can their authors be expected to know everything. Textbook writers have a lot to cover and we can't expect them to have read much on Rockefeller. Unfortunately, they also don't seem to be very familiar with the books on Vanderbilt, Hill, Schwab and other entrepreneurs.[8] None of the twenty texts that I looked at describe the federal aid to steamships and the competition between the subsidized lines and Vanderbilt. Similarly, none of the textbooks mentions Schwab's triumph over the government-run armor plant in West Virginia. The story of the Scrantons is also absent.

Some of the textbook authors do talk about Hill and his accomplishments. In fact, large sections of Bailey's, Garraty's, and Woodward's books tell us about the transcontinental railroads. But the problem of the government subsidies is often not well-reasoned. Bailey, for example, admits that Hill was "probably the greatest railroad builder of all." Bailey even displays a picture of all four transcontinentals and says that Hill's Great Northern was "the only one constructed without lavish federal subsidies." But from this, he does not consider the possibility that federal subsidies may not have been needed. Instead, he says, "Transcontinental railroad building was so costly and risky as to require government subsidies." As we have seen earlier, however, when the federal aid to railroads came, so did political entrepreneurship and corruption. Bailey describes some of this boondoggling and blames not the government, for making federal aid available, but the "grasping railroads" and "greedy corporations," for receiving it.[9]

Bailey later applauds the passing of the Sherman Anti-trust Act and the creation of the Interstate Commerce Commission.

> Not until 1914 were the paper jaws of the Sherman Act fitted with reasonably sharp teeth. Until then, there was some question whether the government would control the trusts or the trusts the government. But the iron grip of monopolistic corporations was being threatened. A revolutionary new principle had been written into the law books by the Sherman Anti-Trust Act of 1890, as well as by the Interstate Com-

merce Act of 1887. Private greed must henceforth be subordinated to public need.[10]

As we have seen, however, the efficient Hill was the one who got hurt by these laws: The Hepburn Act, which strengthened the Interstate Commerce Commission, throttled his international railroad and shipping business; the Sherman Act was used to break up his Northern Securities Company.

Not all historians accept the modified robber-baron view dominant in the textbooks. Specialists in business history have been moving away from this view since the 1960s. Instead, many of them have adopted an interpretation called the "organizational view" of the rise of big business. Where the authors of these textbooks say that entrepreneurs cheated us, organizational historians say that entrepreneurs were not very significant. Business institutions, and their evolution, were more important than the men who ran them. To organizational historians, the rise of the corporation is the central event of the industrial revolution. The corporation—its layers of specialized bureaucracy, its centralization of power, and its thrust to control knowledge—evolved to meet the new challenges in marketing, producing, and distributing goods. In this view, of course, moral questions are not so relevant. The entrepreneur's strategy was almost predetermined by the structure of the industry and the peculiarities of vertical integration. The corporation was bigger than the entrepreneur.[11]

The organizational historians have contributed much to the writing of business history. Their amoral emphasis on the corporation is a refreshing change from the Robber Baron model. Yet, this points up a problem as well. Amoral organizational history has a deterministic quality to it. The structure of the corporation shapes the strategy of the business. In this setting, there is little room for entrepreneurship. Whatever happened had to happen. And if any entrepreneur had not done what he did, another would have come along and done roughly the same thing.

This point of view is perhaps most boldly stated by Robert Thomas:

> Individual entrepreneurs, whether alone or as archetypes, *don't matter*! (Thomas's emphasis) And if indeed they do not matter, the reason, I suggest, is that the supply of entrepreneurs throughout American history, combined with institutions that permitted—indeed fostered—intense competition, was sufficiently elastic to reduce the importance of any particular individual. . . . This is not to argue that innovations

don't matter, only that they do not come about as the product of individual genius but rather as the result of more general forces acting in the economy.[12]

Thomas illustrates his view in the following way:

> Let us examine an analogy from track and field; a close race in the 100-yard dash has resulted in a winner in 9.6 seconds, second place goes to a man whose time is 9.7, and the remaining six runners are clustered below that time. Had the winner instead not been entered in the race and everyone merely moved up a place in the standings, I would argue that it would only make a marginal difference to the spectators. To be sure they would be poorer because they would have had to wait one-tenth of a second longer to determine the winner, but how significant a cost is that? That is precisely the entrepreneurial historian's task, to place the contributions of the entrepreneur within a marginal framework.[13]

It is only when we extend Thomas' logic that we see its flaws. For, in fact, small margins are frequently the crucial difference between success and failure, between genius and mediocrity. To continue the sports analogies, the difference between hitting the ball 311 feet and 312 feet to left field in Yankee stadium is probably the difference between a long out and a home run. The difference between a quarterback throwing a pass forty yards or forty-one yards may be the difference between a touchdown and an incompleted pass. When facing a ten-foot putt, any duffer can hit the ball nine or eleven feet; it takes a pro to consistently sink it.

In the same way small margins can reveal the differences between an entrepreneur, with his creative mind and innovative spirit, and a run-of-the-mill businessman. John D. Rockefeller dominated oil refining primarily by making a series of small cuts in cost. For example, he cut the drops of solder used to seal oil cans from forty to thirty-nine. This small reduction improved his competitive edge: he gained dominance over the whole industry because he was able to sell kerosene at less than eight cents a gallon.

A better illustration would be the small gradual cost-cutting that allowed America to capture foreign steel markets. When Andrew Carnegie entered steel production in 1872, England dominated world production and the price of steel was $56 per ton. By 1900, Carnegie Steel, headed by Charles Schwab, was manufacturing steel for $11.50 per ton—and outstripping the entire production of England. That allowed railroad entrepreneur James J. Hill to buy cheap American rails, ship them across the continent and over the ocean to Japan, and still outprice England. The point here is that America did not claim these markets by natural advantages: they had to be won in international competition by entrepreneurs with vision for an industry and ability to improve products bit by bit.[14]

It would be silly for someone to say that if Carnegie had not come along, someone else would have emerged to singlehandedly outproduce the country that had led the world in steel. Yet some organizational historians say exactly this. They are right in claiming that the rise of the corporation made some of Carnegie's success possible. But Carnegie was the only steel operator before Schwab to take full advantage of this rise. They are also right in saying that the environment (*e. g.* location and resources) plays some role in success. But Carnegie rose to the top *before* the opening of America's Mesabi iron range. American steel companies began outdistancing the British even when the Americans had to import some of their raw material from Cuba and Chile, manufacture it in Pennsylvania, and ship it across the country and over oceans to foreign markets.

This is not to denigrate the organizational view, but only to recognize its limitations. By focusing on the rise of the corporation, organizational historians have shown how corporate structure pervaded and helped to shape American economic and social life. However, the organizational view, like all other interpretations, can't explain everything. Specifically, it tends to ignore or downgrade the significant and unique contributions that entrepreneurs made to American economic development.

The "organizational" and "robber baron" views both have some merit. The rise of the corporation did shape economic development in important ways. Also, we did have industrialists, such as Jay Gould and Henry Villard, who mulcted government money, erected shoddy enterprises, and ran them into the ground. What is missing are the builders who took the risks, overcame strong foreign competition, and pushed American industries to places of world leadership. These entrepreneurs are a major part of the story of American business.

Many historians know this and teach it, but the issue is often muddled because textbooks tend to lump the predators and political adventurers with the creators and builders. Therefore, the teaching ends up like this: "Entrepreneurs cut costs and made many contributions to American economic growth, but they also marred political life by bribing politicians, forming pools, and misusing government funds. Therefore, we needed the federal government to come in and regulate business."

Historians' misconceptions about entrepreneurs have led to problems in related areas as well. This is nowhere more apparent than in the studies of social mobility, which have become very popular among historians ever since the 1960s. Naturally, historians of social mobility have not operated in a vacuum. They have often been influenced by the prevailing historical theories denigrating the role of entrepreneurs and championing the role of government regulation. Put another way, if America's industrial entrepreneurs were a sordid group of replaceable people, then they could not have helped, and may have hindered, upward social mobility in cities throughout America. This is the implicit assumption in many social mobility studies conducted in the last generation.

Influenced by these prevailing views, many historians have argued two basic ideas about social mobility under American capitalism. First is the notion of low social mobility for manual laborers. In *Poverty and Progress: Social Mobility in a Nineteenth Century City*, Stephan Thernstrom finds that "the common workman who remained in Newburyport, [Massachusetts, from] 1850 to 1880 had only a slight chance of rising into a middle class occupation." As for the captains of industry at the opposite end of the spectrum, the second idea is that they usually got rich because they were born rich. This again suggests little mobility. For example, William Miller, recorded the social origins of 190 corporation presidents between 1900–1910. He found that almost 80 percent of them had business or white collar professionals as fathers. More recently, Edward Pessen has argued that 90 percent of the antebellum elite in New York, Philadelphia, and Boston was silk-stocking in origin.[15]

Fortunately, more careful research has discredited this negative view of social mobility. Newburyport, for example, was a stagnant town during the thirty years covered by Thernstrom's research. If new industries were rare and if opportunities were few, then, of course, we would expect social mobility to be low. Michael Weber sensed this and did a study of social mobility in Warren, Pennsylvania, an oil-producing boom town from 1880 to 1910. In Warren, population multiplied every decade as market entrepreneurs created a climate for opportunity and growth. Growth and opportunity seem to have gone together: Warren residents were much more upwardly mobile than those living in Thernstrom's Newburyport.[16]

Flaws are also apparent in William Miller's analysis of the social origins of America's corporate elite in 1910. Miller traced the background of 190 corporate presidents and board chairmen. But as diligent as his research was, he could not discover the social origins of 23 (12 percent) of these men. Miller draws no inference from this lack of evidence. If they left no record, however, the fathers were probably artisans at best, crooks at worst. Furthermore, 60 percent of Miller's industrialists came from farms or small towns (under 8,000 population). This almost certainly makes their fathers country merchants rather than urban capitalists. And the ascent from son of a country merchant to corporate president is indeed sensational. Miller's statistics do not "speak for themselves": they need careful thought and imaginative interpretation.

Newer studies suggest this too. For example, Herbert Gutman found that most of the successful locomotive, iron, and machinery manufacturers in Paterson, New Jersey, started work as apprentice craftsmen or iron workers. Also important is Bernard Saracheck's analysis of a group of entrepreneurs similar in size and prestige to Miller's sample. Saracheck went to "published biographies and company histories" to get a large list of entrepreneurs in a wide range of industries. His group was much more upwardly mobile than Miller's group. Almost one-half of Saracheck's entrepreneurs had fathers who were workers or farmers. Of course the business ties from father to son link many of Saracheck's men, too.[17] But shouldn't this be expected? The key point here is that an open and growing system produces fluidity: manual laborers often became skilled workers or clerks and, for some, there was room at the top.

We still need to explain the contrasting results of Miller and Saracheck. Many of Miller's men were presidents of textile corporations or railroads, both of which were older and even declining fields by 1910. As economist Ralph Andreano has noted, Miller's sample neglected men from newer, more rapidly growing industries such as oil, beverages, and publishing—where Jews and immigrants often excelled.[18] Saracheck included a wider range of businessmen than Miller did, and perhaps for this reason he got a more upwardly mobile group. Again we get the strong tie between rapid growth (this time in industries, not cities) and upward mobility. The work of Edward Pessen has supported the idea that it was easy for rich men and their children to keep their wealth and influence over time. After studying New York City, Philadelphia, Brooklyn, and Boston, Pessen concluded:

> The rich with few exceptions had been born to wealth and comfort, owing their worldly success mostly to inheritance and family support. Instead of rising and falling at a mercurial rate, fortunes usually remained in the hands of their accumulators, whether in the long or the short. . . . Antebellum urban society [and, by implication, postbellum urban society] was very much a class society.[19]

Is there any way to reconcile the stability of wealth found by Pessen and others[20] with the fluid mobility of the Scranton elite? One problem, of course, is with technique and method. Defining who constituted a "leader," an "entrepreneur," or an "industrialist" varies from study to study. A bigger problem is the scope of the research of Pessen and others. In studying the continuity of wealth and talent in families over time, Pessen and others rarely look at all family members, only those who were successful. In fact, if my Scranton research is on target, the successful seem to be the exception, not the rule.

First glances can be deceptive. In Scranton, for example, James Blair and brothers Thomas and George Dickson held three of the five directorships of the First National Bank in 1880. In 1869, James Linen, a nephew of Thomas and George Dickson, married Blair's daughter, Anna; in 1891, Linen became president of the bank for a twenty-two year stretch. To the casual observer, such an occurrence illustrates overpowering continuity of leadership. However, if one looks at all eight sons of Blair and the two Dicksons, a sharply etched picture of failure clearly emerges. Seven of their eight sons never darkened the door of a corporate boardroom; under the eighth, the Dickson Manufacturing Company disintegrated. Continuity from father to son may actually have been the undoing of the business. Furthermore, H. A. Coursen, like bank president James Linen, married a daughter of James Blair; yet Coursen remained a small retailer with no apparent economic influence. In the city of Scranton, at least, the scions of power were not the men their fathers were. Before historians can assert the continuity of economic leadership or family wealth, they must study all the children of the rich, not just the rare conspicuous successes.

A few historians have already been doing this. Lee Benson has studied the Philadelphia economic elite in the 1800s and finds it to be fluid with much upward and downward mobility at all levels. Fredric C. Jaher also finds the "upper strata" in several industrial cities to be very fluid. Stanley Lebergott has studied corporate leadership in America and cites a high rate of discontinuity from father to son.[21] Naturally those born into wealth are, on the whole, more successful than those born into poverty. But to say this is merely to confirm what applies to all societies at all times. Yes, wealth counts; but so do talent, vision, initiative, and luck.

The classic question asked by those historians who study social stratification is this: "Who gets what and why?" We can see how many historians err when they assume that the rich got rich by being robber barons and stayed rich by keeping the corporation in the family and keeping newcomers out of their group as much as possible.

There is another realm of misunderstanding, too: some historians have implied that the economic pie was fixed. This is a weakness in many historical studies of social stratification. Edward Pessen, for example, tells how only one percent of the population held about forty percent of the wealth in many industrial cities in the 1840s. His research is careful, and he insists this share increased over time. Along similar lines, Gabriel Kolko has recorded the distribution of income from 1910 to 1959. He points out that the top one-tenth of Americans usually earned about thirty percent of the national income and that the lowest one-tenth consistently earned only about one percent.[22] This may be true, but Pessen and Kolko also need to emphasize that the total amount of wealth in American society increased geometrically after 1820. This means that American workers improved their standard of living over time even though their percentage of the national income may not have increased. We must also remember that there was constant individual movement up and down the economic ladder. Therefore, the pattern of inequality may have persisted, but the categories of wealth-holding were still fluid in our open society. Finally, it needs to be stressed that one percent of the population often *created* not only their own wealth, but many of the opportunities that enabled others to acquire wealth.

To sum up, then, we need to divide industrialists into two groups. First, were market entrepreneurs, such as Vanderbilt, Hill, the Scrantons, Schwab, Rockefeller, and Mellon, who usually innovated, cut costs, and competed effectively in an open economy. Second, were political entrepreneurs, such as Edward Collins, Henry Villard, Elbert Gary, and Union Pacific builders, all of whom tried to succeed primarily through federal aid, pools, vote-buying, or stock speculation. Market entrepreneurs made decisive and unique contributions to American economic development. The political entrepreneurs stifled productivity (through monopolies and pools), corrupted business and politics, and dulled America's competitive edge.[23]

The second point is that, in the key industries we have studied, the state failed as an economic developer. It failed first as a subsidizer of industrial growth. Vanderbilt showed this in his triumph over the Edward Collins' fleet and the Pacific Mail Steamship Company in the 1850s. James J. Hill showed this forty years later when his privately built Great Northern outdistanced the subsidized Northern Pacific and Union Pacific. The state next failed in the role of an entrepreneur when it tried to build and operate an armor plant in competition with Charles Schwab and Bethlehem Steel. The state also seems to have failed as an active regulator of trade. The evidence in this study is far from conclusive; but we can see problems with the Interstate Commerce Commission and the Sherman Anti-trust Act, both of which were used against the efficient Hill and Rockefeller.

A third point is that the relative absence of state involvement—either through subsidies, tariffs, or income taxes—may have spurred entrepreneurship in the 1840–1920 period. One of the traditional arguments cited by some businessmen, especially the political entrepreneurs, is that a tariff or a subsidy given to a new industry will help that industry survive and eventually flourish against foreign competition. What really happened, though, is that, when Collins and Cunard got subsidies from their governments, they did not become efficient steamship operators; instead, they became lavish wastrels and soon came back asking for larger subsidies, which they then used to compete against more efficient rivals.

In the case of protective tariffs, neither George Scranton or John D. Rockefeller needed them in establishing their steel and oil companies. The Scranton group very profitably built America's first large quantity of rails in a time of a low tariff on British iron imports. Also Rockefeller never needed a tariff (though a small one did exist) on his way to becoming the largest oil producer in the world.

The American government also resisted the temptation to tax large incomes for most of the 1840–1920 period. Low taxes often spur entrepreneurs to invest and take risks. If the builders can keep most of what they build, they will have an incentive to build more. It is true that the state lost the revenue it could have raised if it had taxed large incomes. This was largely offset, however, by the philanthropy of the entrepreneurs. When the income tax became law in 1913, the most anyone had to pay was seven percent of that year's income. Most people paid no tax or only one percent of their earnings. In the years before and after 1913, however, John D. Rockefeller sometimes gave over 50 percent of his annual income to charitable causes. He almost always gave more than ten percent. Hill, Vanderbilt, the Scranton group, and Schwab were also active givers. Sometimes they gave direct gifts to specific people. Usually, though, they used their money to create opportunities that many could exploit. In academic jargon, they tried to improve the infrastructure of the nation by investing in human capital. A case in point consisted of the many gifts to high schools and universities, north and south, black and white, urban and rural. Cheap high-quality education meant opportunities for upwardly mobile Americans, and was also a guarantee that the United States would have quality leadership in its next generation. Vanderbilt University, the University of Chicago, Tuskegee Institute, and Lehigh University were just some of the dozens of schools that were supported by these five entrepreneurs.

Libraries were also sources of support. Not just Andrew Carnegie, but also Hill and Rockefeller were builders and suppliers of libraries. The free public library, which became an American institution in the 1800s, gave opportunities to rich and poor alike to improve their minds and their careers.

Finally, America has always been a farming nation: Rockefeller attacked and helped conquer the boll weevil in the South; Hill helped create dry farming and mixed agriculture in the North. America's cotton and wheat farmers took great advantage of these changes to lead the world in the producing of these two crops.

All of these men (except for Schwab) tried to promote self-help with their giving. They gave to those people or institutions who showed a desire to succeed and a willingness to work. Rockefeller and Hill both paid consultants to sort out the deadbeats and the gold diggers. They sympathized with the needy, but supported only those needy imbued with the work ethic.

Each entrepreneur, of course, had his own variations on the giving theme. Vanderbilt, for example, plowed a series of large gifts into Vanderbilt University and helped make it one of the finest schools in the nation. He almost never gave to individuals, though, and said if he ever did he would have people lined up for blocks to pick his pockets. Schwab, by contrast, was a frivolous giver and had dozens of friends and hangers-on who tapped him regularly for handouts. Rockefeller concentrated his giving in the South and the Midwest; the Scranton group and Schwab focused on the East; Hill gave mainly in the Northwest.

Even without an income or an inheritance tax, these entrepreneurs, and others, had trouble handing down their wealth to the next generation. This was true in part, of course, because they gave so much of it away. As we have seen with the Scranton group, though, most entrepreneurs did not have sons with the same talents the fathers had. Vanderbilt's son William was a worthy successor, but the rest of his children showed little aptitude for business. Hill's three sons did not come close to matching their father's accomplishments; one son, Louis, followed his father as president of the Great Northern, but Louis' career was lackluster. The *Oregonian* of Portland called him "impulsive"; not so much a railroad man, but "a painter of some ability."[24] Charles Schwab and his wife were childless, which was probably fortunate because he squandered over $30 million and died a debtor. Rockefeller's only son, John D. Jr., became a full-time philanthropist. Granted, the senior Rockefeller's five grandsons were all multimillionaires, but their economic influence was much less than that of their grandfather. Sometimes the descendants of these original entrepreneurs parlayed their family names and what was left of their fortunes into political careers. During the 1960s, two of the grandchildren of John D. Rockefeller and one of the great grandchildren of Joseph Scranton were governors of New York, Arkansas and Pennsylvania.[25]

If we seriously study entrepreneurs, the state, and the rise of big business in the United States we will have to sacrifice the textbook morality play of "greedy businessmen" fleecing the public until at last they are stopped by the actions of the state. But, in return, we will have a better understanding of the past and a sounder basis for building our future.

Notes to Chapters

Notes to Chapter One

Commodore Vanderbilt and the Steamship Industry

[1]The literature on the "Robber Barons" controversy is extensive. For a good description of the various arguments, see Glenn Porter, *The Rise of Big Business, 1860–1910* (Arlington Heights, Ill.: AHM Publishing Corporation, 1973).

[2]No recent historian has systematically traced the history of the American steamship industry. Two older histories are David B. Tyler, *Steam Conquers the Atlantic* (New York: D. Appleton-Century Co., 1939); and John G. B. Hutchins, *The American Maritime Industries and Public Policy, 1789–1914* (Cambridge, Mass.: Harvard University Press, 1941).

[3]Modern historians have usually de-emphasized entrepreneurs in describing American industrial development. For a more detailed look at this dichotomy between political and market entrepreneurs, see my book *Urban Capitalists* (Baltimore: Johns Hopkins University Press, 1981). See also Maury Klein, "The Robber Barons," *American History Illustrated* (October 1971), 13–22.

[4]Fulton's monopoly rights are clearly spelled out in a pamphlet entitled *The Right of a State to Grant Exclusive Privileges in Roads, Bridges, Canals, Navigable Waters, etc. Vindicated by a Candid Examination of the Grant from the State of New York to and Contract with Robert R. Livingston and Robert Fulton for Exclusive Navigation* (New York: E. Conrad, 1811). For a good description of the steamboat monopoly, see Maurice G. Baxter, *The Steamboat Monopoly: Gibbons v.Ogden, 1824* (New York: Alfred A. Knopf, 1972), 3-25. See also John S. Morgan, *Robert Fulton* (New York: Mason/Charter, 1977), 178–88.

[5]Baxter, *Gibbons v. Ogden*, 25–26; and Robert G. Albion, "Thomas Gibbons" and "Aaron Ogden," *Dictionary of American Biography*, 20 vols. (New York: Charles Scribner's Sons, 1928–37). 7:242-43; 8:636-37 (hereafter cited

as *DAB*). The best studies of Vanderbilt are Wheaton J. Lane, *Commodore Vanderbilt: An Epic of the Steam Age* (New York: Alfred A. Knopf, 1942); and William A. Croffut, *The Vanderbilts and the Story of Their Fortune* (Chicago: Belford Clarke, 1886). A more recent study of the whole Vanderbilt family is Edwin P. Hoyt, *The Vanderbilts and Their Fortunes* (Garden City, N.Y.: Doubleday, 1962).

[6]Chief Justice Marshall's written decision has been reprinted in John Roche, ed.,*John Marshall: Major Opinions and Other Writings* (Indianapolis: Bobbs-Merrill, 1967), 206–25. A lively account of the *Gibbons v. Ogden* case is in Albert J. Beveridge, *The Life of John Marshall*, 4 vols. (Boston and New York: Houghton, Mifflin and Co., 1916–19), 4:397–460. See also Baxter, *Gibbons v. Ogden*, 37–86; David W. Thomason, "The Great Steamboat Monopoly," *American Neptune* 16 (January and October 1956), 23–40, 279–80; George Dangerfield, "Steamboats' Charter of Freedom: Gibbons vs. Ogden,"*American Heritage* (October 1963), 38–43, 78–80; and Robert G. Albion, *The Rise of New York Port* (New York: Charles Scribner's Sons, 1939), 152–55. For a newer study, see Erik F. Haites, James Mak, and Gary M. Walton, *Western River Transportation: The Era of Internal Development, 1810–1860* (Baltimore: Johns Hopkins University Press, 1975).

[7]David L. Buckman *Old Steamboat Days on the Hudson River* (New York: Grafton Press, 1907), 53–55.

[8]Lane, *Vanderbilt*, 43–49; Morgan, *Fulton*, 179, 187; and Albion, *New York*, 152–55.

[9]Lane, *Vanderbilt*, 47, 50–51.

[10]Albion, *New York*, 154–55; and Lane, *Vanderbilt*, 56–62.

[11]*Harper's Weekly*, March 5, 1859, 145–46; Lane, *Vanderbilt*, 50–84, 231; Albion, *New York*, 156–57.

[12]Sailing ships (called "packets") and clipper ships were still competitive carriers of freight (not passengers) before 1860. Their reliance on wind, not coal, made them cheaper, if not faster. During the 1850s, clipper ships captured a lot of trade to the Orient. The most thorough account of steamships is William S. Lindsay, *History of Merchant Shipping and Ancient Commerce*, 4 vols. (London: Sampson, Marston, Low, and Searle, 1874). See also Hutchins, *The American Maritime Industries*, 348–62.

[13]For a good history of the Cunard line, see Francis E. Hyde, *Cunard and the North Atlantic, 1840–1973* (Atlantic Highlands, N.J.: Humanities Press, 1975). See also Tyler, *Steam Conquers the Atlantic* 142–45; Royal Meeker, *History of the Shipping Subsidies* (New York: Macmillan, 1905), 5–7; Hutchins, *American Maritime Industries*, 349; and Lindsay, *Merchant Shipping*, 4:184. For an excellent critique of shipping subsidies, see Walter T. Dunmore, *Ship*

Subsidies: An Economic Study of the Policy of Subsidizing Merchant Marines (Bostons: Houghton, Mifflin and Co., 1907), esp. 92–103.

[14]*Congressional Globe*, 33rd Congress, 2nd session, 755–56. Cunard later began weekly mail and passenger service. See also Tyler, *Steam Conquers the Atlantic*, 136–48; and William E. Bennet, *The Collins Story* (London: R. Hale, 1957).

[15]For a defense of mail subsidies, see "Speech of James A. Bayard of Delaware on the Collins Line of Steamers Delivered in the Senate of the United Staes, May 10, 1852" (Washington: John T. Towers, 1852). See also Thomas Rainey, *Ocean Steam Navigation and the Ocean Port* (New York: D. Appleton and Co., 1858). For other views of the subsidies, see Lindsay, *Merchant Shipping*, 4:200–03; Hutchins, *American Maritime Industries*, 358–62; and Dunmore, *Ship Subsidies*, 96–103.

[16]French E. Chadwick, *Ocean Steamships* (New York: Charles Scribner's Sons, 1891), 120–22; John H. Morrison, *History of American Steam Navigation* (New York: W. F. Sametz and Co., 1903), 420–23; and N. A., "A Few Suggestions Respecting the United States Steam Mail Service" (n. p., 1850), 9–17.

[17]Tyler, *Steam Conquers the Atlantic*, 202–14; and George E. Hargest, *History of Letter Post Communications Between the United States and Europe, 1845–1875* (Washington: Smithsonian Institution Press, 1971).

[18]*Congressional Globe*, 33rd Congress, Appendix, 192. See also Lane, *Vanderbilt*, 143–44.

[19]President Franklin Pierce vetoed the Collins subsidy bill. He argued that the effect of such a "donation . . . would be to deprive commercial enterprises of the benefits of free competition, and to establish a monopoly, in violation of the soundest principles of public policy, and of doubtful compatibility with the Constitution." *Congressional Globe*, 33rd Congress, 2nd session, 1156–57. But Congress got the whole subsidy back for Collins later in a Navy appropriations bill. See Tyler,*Steam Conquers the Atlantic*, 225–29; Lane, *Vanderbilt*, 143–48; Hutchins, *American Maritime Industries*, 367; Dunmore, *Ship Subsidies*, 92–103; and Roy Nichols, *Franklin Pierce* (Philadelphia: University of Pennsylvania Press, 1958), 377. For Seward's comment, see *Congressional Globe*, 33rd Congress, Appendix, 301.

[20]New York *Tribune*, March 8, 1855; Lane, *Vanderbilt*, 147–48, 150.

[21]Lane, *Vanderbilt*, 147–48. In a letter to the New York *Tribune*, March 8, 1855, Vanderbilt complained that the Collins subsidy was "paralyzing private enterprise, and in fact forbidding it access to the ocean."

[22]Lane, *Vanderbilt*, 148–51, 167; Tyler, *Steam Conquers the Atlantic*, 238–41.

[23]*Congressional Globe*, 35th Congress, 1st session, 2826, 2827, 2843. See also Tyler, *Steam Conquers the Atlantic*, 231–46; James D. McCabe, Jr., *Great Fortunes* (Philadelphia: G. MacLean, 1871); and Meeker, *Shipping Subsidies*, 156.

[24]Lane, *Vanderbilt*, 151–56; and Meeker, *Shipping Subsidies*, 5–20.

[25]Meeker, *Shipping Subsidies*, 10–11; Henry Fry, *The History of North Atlantic Steam Navigation* (New York: Charles Scribner's Sons, 1896), 42–53, 77–78, 81; and Hyde, *Cunard*, 27–34.

[26]Robert Macfarlane, *History of Propellers and Steam Navigation* (New York: George P. Putnam, 1851); Tyler, *Steam Conquers the Atlantic*, 117–18, 138–42; Lane, *Vanderbilt*, 93–94.

[27]*Congressional Globe*, 33rd Congress, Appendix, 354–55; Tyler, *Steam Conquers the Atlantic*, 128–32, 138–42; Lane, *Vanderbilt*, 175–78.

[28]Earnest A. Wiltsee, *Gold Rush Steamers* (San Francisco: Grabhorn Press, 1938), 50–89; Lane, *Vanderbilt*, 85–107; Hutchins, *American Maritime Industries*, 359–60.

[29]Hutchins, *American Maritime Industries*, 359–63.

[30]Lane, *Vanderbilt*, 108–38; Wiltsee, *Gold Rush Steamers*, 112–51.

[31]Lane, *Vanderbilt*, 123–24, 135; and William D. Scroggs, "William Walker," *DAB*, 19:363–65.

[32]*Congressional Globe*, 35th Congress, 1st session, 2843–44.

[33]Lane, *Vanderbilt*, 124, 136.

[34]In 1855, with Vanderbilt paid off, the California lines raised the New York to San Francisco fare from $150 to $300. They also doubled the steerage fare from $75 to $150. Many passengers—real and potential—were angry, but one point needs to be made. This fare was only one-half of what it was before Vanderbilt arrived. The effect of Vanderbilt's competition was to shrink the fare from $600 to $150; when he left, it was still only $300.

For the California lines to have raised the fare any higher would have probably meant two things: first, a decline in the number of passengers wanting to go to California; second, the appearance of a new rival ready to cut fares and capture what traffic was left. Since the California lines had only one-fourth of their subsidy left, they could ill-afford the arrival of another Vanderbilt, so they kept the fares moderately low. See Wiltsee, *Gold Rush Steamers*, 21–26, 55–56, 139–42, 149.

[35]Meeker, *Shipping Subsidies*, 156.

[36]Harry H. Pierce, *Railroads of New York: A Study of Government Aid, 1826–1875* (Cambridge, Mass.: Harvard University Press, 1953), 14–16; George Rogers Taylor, *The Transportation Revolution* (New York: Harper and Row, 1951), 128–31; Julius Rubin, *Canal or Railroad? Imitation and Innovation in*

Response to the Erie Canal in Philadelphia, Baltimore, and Boston (Philadelphia: American Philosophical Society, 1961); Douglass C. North, *Growth and Welfare in the American Past* (Englewood Cliffs, N.J.: Prentice-Hall, 1974). After the Civil War, Vanderbilt sold his steamships and began building the New York Central Railroad from New York to Chicago. Vanderbilt again had to battle political entrepreneurs (this time city councilmen and state legislators) in New York who demanded bribes from Vanderbilt before they would approve of a right-of-way for his railroad. But Vanderbilt never took his eyes off the main task: building the best railroad and delivering goods at the lowest possible prices. He spearheaded America's switch from iron to steel rails, standardized his railroad's gauge, and experimented with the four track system. He improved roadbeds and rolling stock and cut his cost in half in seven years—all the time maintaining an eight percent dividend to stockholders.

Notes to Chapter Two

James J. Hill and the Transcontinental Railroads

[1]John A. Garraty, *The American Nation: A History of the United States*, 7th ed. (New York: Harper Collins, 1991), 497.

[2]James F. Stover, *American Railroads* (Chicago: University of Chicago Press, 1961), 67; Henry Kirke White, *History of the Union Pacific Railway* (Chicago: University of Chicago Press, 1895).

[3]Robert G. Athearn, *Union Pacific Country* (Chicago: Rand McNally, 1971), 37–38, 43–44.

[4]J. R. Perkins, *Trails, Rails, and War: The Life of General G. M. Dodge* (Indianapolis: Bobbs-Merrill, 1929), 207. See also Stanley P. Hirshson, *Grenville M. Dodge: Soldier, Politician, Railroad Pioneer* (Bloomington, Ind.: Indiana University Press, 1967)

[5]Athearn, *Union Pacific Country*, 200–03.

[6]Perkins, *Dodge*, 231–33, 238. See also William F. Rae, *Westward By Rail: The New Route to the East* (London: Longmans, Green, and Co., 1871).

[7]Athearn, *Union Pacific Country*, 139–42.

[8]Perkins, *Dodge*, 205–06; Athearn, *Union Pacific Country*, 153.

[9]Athearn, *Union Pacific Country*, 224, 337–40, 346.

[10]Julius Grodinsky, *Transcontinental Railway Strategy, 1869–1893: A Study of Businessmen* (Philadelphia: University of Pennsylvania Press, 1962), 70–71.

[11]For a full description of the Central Pacific, see Oscar Lewis,*The Big Four: The Story of Huntington, Stanford, Hopkins, and Crocker,and of the Building of the Central Pacific* (New York: Alfred A. Knopf. 1938).

[12]Grodinsky, *Transcontinental Railway Strategy*, 137. For A fuller account of Villard's career, see James B. Hedges, *Henry Villard and the Railways of the Northwest* (New Haven: Yale University Press, 1930).

[13] Hedges, *Villard*, 112–211; Grodinsky, *Transcontinental Railway Strategy*, 140, 185.

[14]Mildred H. Comfort, *James Jerome Hill, Railroad Pioneer* (Minneapolis: T. S. Denison, 1973), 64–65.

[15]Grodinsky, *Transcontinental Railway Strategy*, 137.

[16]Albro Martin, *James J. Hill and the Opening of the Northwest* (New York: Oxford University Press, 1976), 16–45; Stewart Holbrook, *James J. Hill: A Great Life in Brief* (New York: Alfred A Knopf, 1955), 9–23.

[17]Stover, *American Railroads*, 76; Holbrook, *Hill*, 13–42.

[18]Martin, *Hill*, 122–40, 161–71, passim; Holbrook, *Hill*, 44, 54–68.

[19]Martin,*Hill*, 183; Robert Sobel, *The Entrepreneurs: Explorations Within the American Business Tradition* (New York: Weybright and Talley, 1974), 140; Howard L. Dickman, "James Jerome Hill and the Agricultural Development of the Northwest" (Ph.D. dissertation, University of Michigan, 1977), 67–144.

[20]Holbrook, *Hill*, 93; Martin, *Hill*, 366.

[21]Martin, *Hill*, 381–83; Comfort, *Hill*, 67–70.

[22]Martin, *Hill*, 233, 236.

[23]*Ibid.*, 225, 239–43, 264–70.

[24]*Ibid.*, 298, 307, 338, 346, 494.

[25]*Ibid.*, 410–11.

[26]*Ibid.*, 300, 414–15, 442.

[27]Robert W. Fogel, *The Union Pacific Railroad* (Baltimore: Johns Hopkins University Press, 1960), 99–100.

[28]*Ibid.*, 25. Carl Degler has a variant of this viewpoint. He says, "In the West, where settlement was sparse, railroad building required government assistance." Later, he adds, "By the time the last of the four pioneer transcontinentals, James J. Hill's Great Northern, was constructed in the 1890s, private capital was able and ready to do the job unassisted by government." This argument suggests that the key variable is the timing of the building, not the subsidy itself. The main problem here is that Hill's transcontinental across the sparse Northwest, especially with the Canadian Pacific above him and the Northern Pacific below him, was just as risky as the Union Pacific was. That's why it was called "Hill's Folly." Also, Hill was building at roughly the same time as the Northern Pacific; but Hill succeeded, while the Northern Pacific failed. Finally, we need to remember that, in 1893, Hill flourished, while the Union Pacific, the Northern Pacific, and the Santa Fe all went into receivership. This brings us back to the subsidy as the problem, not the timing of the gift. See Carl Degler, *The Age of the Economic Revolution, 1876–1900* (Glenview, Ill.: Scott, Foresman and Co., 1977), 19–20.

[29]For a development of much of this argument, see Albro Martin, *Enterprise Denied: Origins of the Decline of American Railroads, 1897–1917* (New

York: Columbia University Press, 1971). See also Martin, *Hill*, 535–44.

[30]Fogel, *Union Pacific Railroad*, 41.

[31]Holbrook, *Hill*, 161–63; Sobel, *Entrepreneurs*, 138; James J. Hill, *Highways of Progress* (New York: Doubleday, Page, and Co., 1910), 156–69.

[32]Holbrook, *Hill*, 162–63.

[33]*Ibid.*, 161; Sobel, *Entrepreneurs*, 135; Martin, *Hill*, 464–65.

[34]Martin, *Hill*, 298–99, 307, 347, 442, 462.

[35]Hill, *Highways of Progress*, 156–184; Holbrook, *Hill*, 163; Ari and Olive Hoogenboom, *A History of the ICC: From Panacea to Palliative* (New York: W. W. Norton, 1976), 49–59.

[36]Hill, *Highways of Progress*, 169; Martin, *Hill*, 540.

[37]Dominick T. Armentano, *The Myths of Antitrust: Economic Theory and Legal Cases* (New Rochelle, N.Y.: Arlington Press, 1972), 56–58.

[38]Martin, *Hill*, 494–523.

[39]Armentano, *The Myths of Antitrust*, 58–62; Martin, *Hill*, 515, 518.

[40]Armentano, *The Myths of Antitrust*, 58–59.

[41]Martin, *Hill*, 519.

[42]Robert Sobel, *The Age of Giant Corporations: A Microeconomic History of American Business, 1914–1970* (Westport, Conn.: Greenwood Press, 1972), 189–94.

Notes to Chapter Three

The Scrantons and America's First Iron Rails

[1]For a good discussion of America's iron industry in the 1830s and 1840s, see Peter Temin, *Iron and Steel in Nineteenth Century America: An Economic Inquiry* (Cambridge, Mass.: MIT Press, 1964), 20–52.

[2]*Ibid.*, 47. Biddle's quotation is in David Craft, W. A. Wilcox, Alfred Hand, and J. Wooldridge, *History of Scranton, Pennsylvania* (Dayton: H. W. Crew, 1891), 247.

[3]America's first rails were built in the 1820s and were made of wood. These were gradually supplemented by English-made iron rails during the 1830s and 1840s. A couple of American firms, particularly the Mount Savage Works at Lonaconing, Maryland, experimented with making iron rails in the 1840s before the Scrantons did. But the Scrantons were the first to mass-produce notable quantities of iron rails. See W. David Lewis, "The Early History of the Lackawanna Iron and Coal Company: A Study in Technological Adaptation," *Pennsylvania Magazine of History and Biography* 96 (October 1972), 456–58; Stover, *American Railroads*, 20–29; John Moody, *The Railroad Builders* (New Haven: Yale University Press, 1919), 66–70; Temin, *Iron and Steel in Nineteenth Century America*, 109, 117.

[4]For a more detailed description of the Scranton experiment, see Folsom, *Urban Capitalists*.

[5]Much information on the Scrantons' efforts at economic development can be gathered from the Scranton papers, known as the Edmund T. Lukens Collection (hereafter cited ETLC), in the Hagley Museum and Library in Wilmington, Delaware. Another smaller collection of Scranton correspondence is available in the Lackawanna Historical Society (hereafter LHS) in Scranton, Pennsylvania. The best secondary source on the Scrantons' early attempts at iron and coal development is Lewis, "The Lackawanna Iron and Coal Company." For the quotation in this paragraph, see William Henry to Selden Scranton, March 8, 1840, Box 9, ETLC.

[6]The trauma of the Scrantons' early years in the Lackawanna Valley is described in the correspondence in Box 9, ETLC. For a good summary of

the Scrantons from 1841–43, see Lewis, "The Lackawanna Iron and Coal Company," 435–51.

[7]Frederick L. Hitchcock, *History of Scranton and Its People*, 2 vols. (New York: Lewis Historical Publishing Co., 1914), 1:28.

[8]*Ibid.*; Personal interviews with Robert C. Mattes, Lackawanna Historical Society, October 1972, and April 1973.

[9]For a good discussion of this, see Lewis, "The Lackawanna Iron and Coal Company."

[10]John P. Gallagher, "Scranton: Industry and Politics, 1835–1885," (Ph.D. dissertation, Catholic University, 1964), 39, 57; Lewis, "The Lackawanna Iron and Coal Company," 454–55; Horace Hollister, *Contributions to the History of the Lackawanna Valley* (New York: W. H. Tinson, 1857), 166.

[11]Edward Hungerford, *Men of Erie: A Story of Human Effort* (New York: Random House, 1946), 76–78; Lewis, "The Lackawanna Iron and Coal Company," 454–55; Hollister, *Contributions*, 166.

[12]Edward H. Mott, *Between Ocean and the Lakes: The Story of Erie* (New York: Ticker Publishing Company, 1908), 91; Benjamin H. Throop, *A Half Century in Scranton* (Scranton, Pa.: Press of the Scranton Republican, 1895), 114–16.

[13]George W. Scranton to Selden Scranton, August 3, 1846, ETLC, Box 9, in Lewis, "The Lackawanna Iron and Coal Company," 460–63. See also Frank W. Taussig, *The Tariff History of the United States*, 7th ed. (New York: G. P. Putnam's Sons, 1923), 112–35. George Scranton later became an advocate for higher tariffs. See the *Daily National Intelligencer*, March 27, 1861.

[14]Hitchcock, *History of Scranton*, 1:51–57. Lewis, "The Lackawanna Iron and Coal Company," 440, 464–66.

[15]Hitchcock, *History of Scranton*, 1:51–57; Report of Joseph J. Albright, coal agent, May 1852, ETLC, Box 11; Joseph H. Scranton to Selden T. Scranton, February 23, 1854, ETLC, Box 11; Charles Silkman to Selden T. Scranton, March 28, 1849, ETLC, Box 13.

[16]Robert J. Casey and W. A. S. Douglas, *The Lackawanna Story: The First Hundred Years of the Delaware, Lackawanna, and Western Railroad* (New York: McGraw-Hill, 1951), 32–72, 208–11; Hitchcock, *History of Scranton* 1:55–57. Michael Meylert to Selden T. Scranton, August 3, 1853, ETLC, Box 13; Horace Hayden, Alfred Hand, and John W. Jordan, *Genealogical and Family History of the Wyoming and Lackawanna Valleys Pennsylvania*, 2 vols. (New York: Lewis Publishing Co., 1906), 2:50–51, 154.

[17]Two of the important New Yorkers were Anson Phelps and William E. Dodge, who founded Phelps, Dodge and Company. See William B. Shaw, "William Earl Dodge," Harold U. Faulkner, "Anson G. Phelps," and Joseph

V. Fuller, "William Walter Phelps," *DAB*, 5:352–53, 14:525–26, and 533; Lewis, "The Lackawanna Iron and Coal Company," 458–59. In a letter to Selden Scranton, John J. Phelps asserted, "The Erie Company is managed by Connecticut businessmen—of large means, and liberal views, and they will be disposed to go for . . . the several interests of their city." See John J. Phelps to Selden T. Scranton, December 16, 29, 1845, ETLC, Box 13; and Hayden et al., *Wyoming and Lackawanna Valleys*, 2:153–54.

[18]William Henry to Selden T. Scranton, March 8, 1840, June 8, July, and August 24, 1841, ETLC, Box 9; Charles Silkman to Selden T. Scranton, March 28, 29, 1849, ETLC, Box 13; Lewis, "The Lackawanna Iron and Coal Company," 442.

[19]Throop, *A Half Century in Scranton*, 135.

[20]This terminology comes from Leo Marx, *The Machine in the Garden: Terminology and the Pastoral Ideal in America* (New York: Oxford University Press, 1964).

.[21]Hollister, *Contributions*, 124–25.

[22]Some members of this committee were upset that the North Branch Canal would not provide a feeder to connect their farming area to outside markets. Wilkes-Barre *Advocate*, December 19, 1838, cited by Hollister, *Contributions*, 105. For an additional description of the opposition to economic development, see Throop, *A Half Century in Scranton*, 124–26.

[23]Horace Hollister, *History of the Lackawanna Valley* (New York: C. A. Alvord, 1869), 238; William Henry to Selden T. Scranton, March 10, 1841, ETLC, Box 9; Sanford Grant to Selden T. Scranton, June 9, 1841, ETLC, Box 9; George W. Scranton to Selden T. Scranton, May 23, 1846, ETLC, Box 9.

[24]Hollister, *Contributions*, 116; Hollister, *History of the Lackawanna Valley*, 231–32; Lewis, "The Lackawanna Iron and Coal Company," 454; Sanford Grant to Selden T. Scranton, June 9, 1841, ETLC, Box 9. One contemporary insisted, "The Lackawanna Iron Works, supposed to be hopelessly bankrupt, were of no account to the old settlers in their struggles for a single gleam of financial sunlight." John R. Durfee, *Reminiscences of Carbondale, Dundaff, and Providence Forty Years Past* (Philadelphia: Miller's Bible Publishing House, 1875), 103.

[25]Hollister, *Contributions*, 108, 118, 124, 133; Throop, *A Half Century in Scranton*, 263–76.

[26]Hitchcock, *History of Scranton*, 1:360–62; Scranton *Republican*, March 30, and April 13, 27, 1866; *The Legislative Record: Debates and Proceedings of the Pennsylvania Legislature, Session of 1866* (Harrisburg, 1866) 825–26.

[27]Scranton *Republican*, April 13, 1866. Henry C. Bradsby, *History of Luzerne County, Pennsylvania, with Biographical Selections* (Chicago: S. B. Nelson and Co., 1893), 473–74, 520.

[28]Durfee, *Reminiscences, et passim;* R. G. Dun Credit Ledgers, Pennsylvania, Luzerne County, 89:49, 53, 71, 89.

[29]W. David Lewis, "William Henry, Armsmaker, Ironmaster, and Railroad Speculator: A Case Study in Failure," in *Proceedings of the Business History Conference* (Ft. Worth, Texas, 1973), 51–94; Manuscript Census Returns, Ninth Census of the United States, 1870, Luzerne County, Pennsylvania, National Archives Microfilm Series, M-593, Roll 1368; Personal interview with Robert C. Mattes, October 1972. See also John H. Frederick, "George Whitfield Scranton," *DAB,* 16:513–14; *Daily National Intelligencer,* March 27, 1861.

[30]The listing of wealth for Scranton, Blair, and Platt is in Manuscript Census Returns, Luzerne County, Pennsylvania, 1870. The quotation is from Joseph H. Scranton to Selden T. Scranton, February 28, 1843, Box 9, ETLC, which is discussed in Lewis, "The Lackawanna Iron and Coal Company," 449.

[31]The information on wealth holding is available in the federal manuscript censuses of 1850 and 1870. The 1870 census citation is in note 29. The 1850 census citation is Manuscript Census Returns, Seventh Census of the United States, 1850, Luzerne County, Pennsylvania, National Archives Microfilm Series, M-432, Roll 793.

[32]This deduction is implied from other studies of city and hinterland. For example, see James W. Livingood, *The Philadelphia-Baltimore Trade Rivalry, 1780–1860* (Harrisburg, Pa.: Pennsylvania Historical and Museum Commission, 1947). A recent study that involves coal and Pennsylvania regions is Edward J. Davies II, *Anthracite Aristocracy: Leadership and Social Change in the Hard Coal Regions of Northeastern Pennsylvania, 1800–1930* (DeKalb, Ill.: Northern Illinois University Press, 1985).

[33]Pennsylvania's Schuylkill region is an example of a coal area that did not develop a strong local elite and became subordinate to nearby Philadelphia. See Davies, *Anthracite Aristocracy.* See also Robert Baldwin, "Patterns of Development in Newly Settled Regions," *Manchester School of Economics and Social Studies* 24 (May 1956) 161–79.

[34]For a more detailed description of Scranton attracting investors from nearby towns, see Folsom, *Urban Capitalists,* chapters 3, 4, and 6.

[35]New York *Sun,* May 10, 1935, in Obituaries Notebook No. 7, in Lackawanna Historical Society, 74; Hitchcock, *History of Scranton* 1:10–13; Throop, *A Half Century in Scranton;* Hollister, *Contributions,* 132–33; Personal interview with Robert C. Mattes, April 1973; Personal interview with William Lewis, July 1978.

[36]Samuel C. Logan, *The Life of Thomas Dickson: A Memorial* (Scranton, Pa.: n.p., 1888); Gerald M. Best, *Locomotives of the Dickson Manufacturing*

Company, (San Marino, Ca.: Golden West, 1966); Chapman Publishing Company, *Portrait and Biographical Record of Lackawanna County, Pennsylvania* (New York: Chapman Publishing Co., 1897), 502–03, 455–57; Hitchcock, *History of Scranton*, 1:89–90; 2:22–24, 37–40, 498–501; R. G. Dun Credit Ledgers, Pennsylvania, Luzerne County, 93:119, 94:330.

[37]Joseph J. Albright to Selden Scranton, July 7, 1850, October 14, 1850, and November 9, 1850, Boxes 36 and 10, ETLC; Chapman Publishing Company, *Lackawanna County*, 205–07.

[38]R. G. Dun Credit Ledgers, Pennsylvania, Luzerne County, 94:40, 91:939; Chapman Publishing Company, *Lackawanna County*, 205–07.

[39]Phillip Walter to Selden T. Scranton, May 19, 1852, ETLC, Box 10; for a brief description of Walter's relationship to the Scrantons, see Hitchcock, *History of Scranton*, 1:7.

[40]The Welshman was Lewis Pughe. See W. W. Munsell and Company, *History of Luzerne, Lackawanna, and Wyoming Counties with Biographical Sketches of Some of their Prominent Men and Pioneers* (New York: W. W. Munsell and Co., 1880), 438D, 392B; Hitchcock, *History of Scranton*, 1:211–12, 426–34.

[41]Hitchcock, *History of Scranton*, 2:1–5. See also Luther Laflin Mills, Joseph H. Twitchell, Alfred Hand, Frederick L. Hitchcock, James H. Torrey, Eugene Smith, Edward B. Sturges, Charles H. Wells, James McLeod, and James A. Beaver, eds., *Henry Martyn Boies: Appreciations of His Life and Character* (New York, 1904).

[42]Thomas F. Murphy, *History of Lackawanna County*, 3 vols. (Topeka: Historical Publishing Co., 1928), 1:614–16.

[43]*Ibid.*, 617–18; Craft et al., *History of Scranton*, 283–84.

[44]In 1900, Scranton's population was 102,026. *Twelfth Census of the United States, 1900: Population* (Washington: Government Printing Office, 1902), 2:606–07.

[45]For a more detailed analysis of this Scranton elite, see Folsom, *Urban Capitalists*, chapter 7.

[46]Personal interviews with Robert C. Mattes, April 1973, and William Lewis, July 1978.

[47]For a fuller discussion of this point, see Burton W. Folsom, "Like Fathers, Unlike Sons: The Fall of the Business Elite in Scranton, Pennsylvania, 1880–1920," *Pennsylvania History* 46 (October 1980), 291–309.

[48]Logan, *Thomas Dickson*; Hitchcock, *History of Scranton*, 1:89–90, 254–55; 2:22–24; Chapman Publishing Company, *Lackawanna County*, 456–57; 502–04; Mills et al., *Henry Martyn Boies*, 51; *Scranton City Directory, 1921*; Murphy, *History of Lackawanna County*, 682–83.

[49]R. G. Dun Credit Ledgers, Pennsylvania, Luzerne County, 95:133, 93:380, 91:1136; Murphy, *History of Lackawanna County*, 1:128–29; Rowland Berthoff, "The Social Order of the Anthracite Region, 1825–1902," *Pennsylvania Magazine of History and Biography* 89 (September 1965), 261–91.

[50]Hitchcock, *History of Scranton* 2:10–13; New York *Sun*, May 10, 1935, cited in Obituaries Notebook No. 7, in Lackawanna Historical Society, 74; Personal interview with Robert C. Mattes, director of the Lackawanna Historical Society, April 1973.

[51]Obituaries Notebook No. 7, in Lackawanna Historical Society, 40; R. G. Dun Credit Ledgers, Pennsylvania, Luzerne County, 96:249.

[52]Hitchcock, *History of Scranton*, 1:254–55; 2:10–13.

[53]Most historians and scholars have argued that continuity from wealthy father to son is typical. See E. Digby Baltzell, *Philadelphia Gentlemen* (Glencoe, Ill.: Free Press, 1958); Edward Pessen, *Riches, Class, and Power Before the Civil War* (Lexington, Mass.: D. C. Heath and Co., 1973); Ferdinand Lundberg, *The Rich and Super-Rich* (New York: Lyle Stuart, 1968); John N. Ingham, *The Iron Barons: A Social Analysis of an American Urban Elite, 1874–1965* (Westport, Conn.: Greenwood Press, 1978).

For a point of view different from these studies, see Lee Benson, Robert Gough, Ira Harkavy, Marc Levine, and Brodie Remington, "Propositions on Economic Strata and Groups, Social Classes, Ruling Classes: A Strategic Natural Experiment, Philadelphia Economic and Prestige Elites, 1775–1860" (unpublished essay, University of Pennsylvania, 1976). My thinking on this issue has been strongly influenced by Professor Benson.

[54]Hitchcock, *History of Scranton*, 2:53–55, 30–32, 5–7, 188–91; *Scranton City Directory, 1920, 1921*.

Notes to Chapter Four

Charles Schwab and the Steel Industry

[1]Charles M. Schwab, *Succeeding With What You Have* (New York: Century Co., 1917), 39–41.

[2]Robert Hessen, *Steel Titan: The Life of Charles M. Schwab* (New York: Oxford University Press, 1975), 4–12 (quotations on pages 10 and 11).

[3]*Ibid.*, 13–16, 21; Eugene G. Grace, *Charles M. Schwab* (n. p., 1947), 6.

[4]Harold Livesay, *Andrew Carnegie* (Boston: Little, Brown and Co., 1975), 101, 165–66.

[5]Hessen, *Schwab*, 70; Joseph Frazier Wall, *Andrew Carnegie* (New York: Oxford University Press, 1970), 665.

[6]Wall, *Carnegie*, 532–33; Livesay, *Carnegie*, 117–18.

[7]Hessen, *Schwab*, 28–30, 41–42, 60.

[8]*Ibid.*, 31, 38, 74.

[9]Wall, *Carnegie*, 330–38; Livesay, *Carnegie*, 101.

[10]Livesay, *Carnegie*, 103.

[11]Wall, *Carnegie*, 329–32, 337, 341–42.

[12]Livesay, *Carnegie*, 150, 165–66; Hessen, *Schwab*, 69–70.

[13]Livesay, *Carnegie*, 187–88.

[14]Hessen, *Schwab*, 123.

[15]*Ibid.*, 125–27 (quotation on page 127). The Finance Committee at U. S. Steel rejected Schwab's request for more ore land. I assume that Gary approved of this decision.

[16]*Ibid.*, 121, 133–40, 299.

[17]*Ibid.*, 119–22, 138.

[18]*Ibid.*, 147–62.

[19]Raymond Walters, *Bethlehem Long Ago and Today* (Bethlehem: Carey Printing Co., 1923), 64; William J. Heller, ed., *History of Northampton County, Pennsylvania, and the Grand Valley of the Lehigh*, 3 vols. (Boston: American Historical Society, 1920), 1:44; Joseph M. Levering, *A History of Bethlehem*,

Pennsylvania, 1741–1892, with Some Account of Its Founders and their Early Activity in America (Bethlehem: Times Publishing Co., 1903), 722–24; Alfred Mathews and Austin N. Hungerford, *History of the Counties of Lehigh and Carbon, in the Commonwealth of Pennsylvania* (Philadelphia: Everts and Richards, 1884), 690, 704–05; John W. Jordan, ed., *Encyclopedia of Pennsylvania Biography*, 32 vols. (New York: Lewis Historical Publishing Co., 1914–1967), 6:2139–42.

[20]John Fritz, *The Autobiography of John Fritz* (New York: J. Wiley and Sons, 1912), 173–74; Hessen, *Schwab*, 164–66.

[21]Hessen, *Schwab*, 165–66.

[22]*Ibid.*, 167–68; Walters, *Bethlehem*, 88.

[23]Hessen, *Schwab*, 170–72, 177–78, 252; Walters, *Bethlehem*, 88.

[24]Hessen, *Schwab*, 169.

[25]*Ibid.*, 171.

[26]*Ibid.*, 185.

[27]*Ibid.*, 226–27, 270, 272, 276.

[28]*Ibid.*, 172–73.

[29]*Ibid.*, 173–75, 182–84.

[30]*Ibid.*, 186–87, 267–69.

[31]*Ibid.*, 230, 265–66; *New York Times*, April 14, 1915; Heller, *History of Northampton County*, 276; and Robert Hessen, "Charles M. Schwab, President of United States Steel, 1901–1904," *Pennsylvania Magazine of History and Biography* 96 (April 1972), 203.

[32]Hessen, *Schwab*, 236–44 (quotation on page 236).

[33]*Ibid.*, 240–44 (quotation on page 244).

[34]My understanding of the armor-plate business in general, and how it affected Bethlehem Steel in particular, has been greatly enriched by reading Hessen, *Schwab*, 42–58, 217–26, 307–10. Reading Hessen has led me to several key sources on the armor-plate issue.

[35]Andrew Carnegie to Josephus Daniels, December 9, 1913, Box 497, Josephus Daniels papers, Library of Congress. See also Robert Seager, "Ten Years Before Mahan: The Unofficial Case for the New Navy, 1880–1890," *Mississippi Valley Historical Review*, 60 (December 1953), 491–512.

[36]For the point of view of the steel companies, see Eugene G. Grace to Josephus Daniels, April 19, 1913, Box 497, Daniels papers; Andrew Carnegie to Daniels, December 9, 1913, in *Ibid.*; Statements by Senators Boies Penrose and Warren G. Harding in the *Congressional Record* in *Ibid.*; New York *Herald*, January 28, 1911, in *Ibid.* For the point of view of the critics of the steel companies, see Benjamin Tillman to Daniels, May 22, 1913, in *Ibid.*; T. B. H.

Stenhouse to Daniels, September 24, 1913, in *Ibid.*; Statement by Representative Clyde Tavenner in *Congressional Record*, in *Ibid.*

See also Melvin I. Urofsky, *Big Steel and the Wilson Administration* (Columbus, Ohio: Ohio State University Press, 1969), 117–51; Hessen, *Schwab*, 42–58, 216–26; Josephus Daniels, *The Wilson Era: Years of Peace, 1910–1917* (Chapel Hill: University of North Carolina Press, 1944), 351–63; Francis B. Simkins, *Pitchfork Ben Tillman: South Carolinian* (Baton Rouge: Louisiana State University Press, 1967), 511–13.

[37]Benjamin Tillman to Josephus Daniels, May 22, 1913; Josephus Daniels' Response to Senate Resolution, July 12, 1913; Andrew Carnegie to Josephus Daniels, December 9, 1913, all in Box 497, Daniels papers. See also Urofsky, *Big Steel*, 136, 142–43.

[38]In 1906, for example, the government took bids for 8000 tons of armor plate. The Carnegie division of U. S. Steel bid $370 per ton, Bethlehem Steel bid $381, and Midvale Steel bid $346. The Navy department divided the contract among all three after U. S. Steel and Bethlehem Steel agreed to Midvale's $346 per ton price. The next year all three companies submitted identical bids of $420 per ton. These $420 per ton bids continued until 1912, and the armor contracts were always divided among all three companies. See extracts from the Report of Hon. Josephus Daniels, Secretary of the Navy, December 1, 1913; Armor Contracts as Awarded for Increase of Navy to Date, January 26, 1915; Eugene Grace to Josephus Daniels, April 19, 1913; Claude Swanson to Woodrow Wilson, March 21, 1916, all in Josephus Daniels papers, Boxes 497 and 498, Library of Congress.

[39]Benjamin Tillman to Josephus Daniels, May 22, 1913; Eugene Grace to Daniels, April 19, 1913; Extracts from the Report of Hon. Josephus Daniels, Secretary of the Navy, December 1, 1913; Claude Swanson to Woodrow Wilson, March 21, 1916, in Josephus Daniels papers, Boxes 497 and 498. See also Benjamin Tillman to Woodrow Wilson, January 5, 1916; March 9, 1916, April 29, 1916, and May 21, 1916; and Josephus Daniels to Wilson, April 12, 1913; Charles Schwab and Eugene Grace, "Should the Government Destroy Private Armor-Making Industries?" April 5, 1916, in Woodrow Wilson papers, microfilm reel 259, Library of Congress.

[40]Tillman's speech to the Senate is in *Congressional Record*, 64th Congress, 1st session, February 8, 1916. Woodrow Wilson to Benjamin Tillman, January 6, 1916, in Wilson papers, microfilm reel 259.

[41]See two articles by Charles Schwab and Eugene Grace. One is untitled; the other is "Should the Government Destroy Private Armor-Making Industries?" April 5, 1916, both in Wilson papers, microfilm reel 259.

[42]Daniels, *Wilson Era*, 360; Hessen, *Schwab*.

[43]C. F. Adams, Secretary of the Navy, to the Chairman of the House Committee on Naval Affairs, National Archives, Record Group 80, Entry 13, Box 141; Claude A. Swanson, Secretary of the Navy, to Henry Wallace, National Archives, Record Group 80, Entry 13, Box 55; William D. Leahy, Acting Secretary of the Navy, to Senator Gerald P. Nye, National Archives, Record Group 80, Entry 13, Box 176. See also George Marvell to Josephus Daniels, February 9, 1921, Daniels papers; and Roger M. Freeman, *The Armor-Plate and Gun Forging Plant of the U. S. Navy Department at South Charleston, West Virginia* (n. p., 1920).

[44]Hessen, *Schwab*, 244.

[45]*Ibid.*, 279–80.

[46]*Ibid.*, 282; Jude Wanniski, *The Way the World Works* (New York: Basic Books, 1978), 116–48; Don McLeod, "The History of Protectionism Proves the Value of Free Trade," *Insight* (June 30, 1986), 11–14.

[47]Hessen, *Schwab*, 280–82.

[48]*Ibid.*, 288–90, 292.

[49]*Ibid.*, 132–33, 285–86, 290–91, 296, 298–300.

[50]*Ibid.*, 293–303.

Notes to Chapter Five

John D. Rockefeller and the Oil Industry

[1]Allan Nevins, *Study in Power: John D. Rockefeller*, 2 vols. (New York: Charles Scribner's Sons, [1940] 1953), 1:672, 208. Nevins was the first historian to look at the wealth of primary source material in the Rockefeller papers (now located in Tarrytown, N.Y.). His thousand-page biography is still the standard work on Rockefeller and was indispensable to me. For differing points of view, see Jules Abels, *The Rockefeller Billions: The Story of the World's Most Stupendous Billions* (New York: Macmillan Company, 1965); Peter Collier and David Horowitz, *The Rockefellers: An American Dynasty* (New York: New American Library, 1976), 3–72; Ferdinand Lundberg, *The Rockefeller Syndrome* (Secaucus, N.J.: Lyle Stuart, 1975); and David Freeman Hawke, *John D.: The Founding Father of the Rockefellers* (New York: Harper and Row, 1980).

[2]Grace Goulder, *John D. Rockefeller: The Cleveland Years* (Cleveland: Western Reserve Historical Society, 1972), 17–25.

[3]*Ibid.*, 26–27; Nevins, *Rockefeller*, 1:43, 100–02.

[4]Nevins, *Rockefeller*, 1:132.

[5]*Ibid.*, 1:103, 186–91; Goulder, *Rockefeller*, 59–73.

[6]For a good discussion of the beginnings of the petroleum industry, see Harold F. Williamson and Arnold R. Daum, *The American Petroleum Industry: The Age of Illumination, 1859–1899* (Evanston, Ill.: Northwestern University Press, 1959), 27–114.

[7]Goulder, *Rockefeller*, 59–80; Nevins, *Rockefeller*, 1:199, 167–69, 173, 205.

[8]Williamson and Daum, *American Petroleum Industry*, 82–194.

[9]Nevins, *Rockefeller*, 1:183–85, 197–98.

[10]*Ibid.*, 1:183–86, 268–70, 289; Williamson and Daum, *American Petroleum Industry*, 342–68; John D. Rockefeller, *Random Reminiscences of Men and Events* (Garden City, N.Y.: Doubleday, Doran, and Co., 1933), 88.

[11]Nevins, *Rockefeller*, 1:666.

[12]*Ibid.*, 1:256, 296–97.

[13]*Ibid.*, 1:115, 175, 279, 487. See Ida M. Tarbell, *The History of the Standard Oil Company*, (New York: Harper and Row, 1966); and Henry Demarest Lloyd, *Wealth Against Commonwealth* (Englewood Cliffs, N.J.: Prentice-Hall, 1963).

[14]Nevins, *Rockefeller*, 1:277–79, 555–56, 671–72.

[15]*Ibid.*, 1:306–37; Williamson and Daum, *American Petroleum Industry*, 342–68.

[16]Rockefeller, *Random Reminiscences*, 55–76.

[17]Nevins, *Rockefeller*, 1:366.

[18]*Ibid.*, 1:380.

[19]*Ibid.*, 2:76; 1:277–79.

[20]*Ibid.*, 2:2–4, 96ff; Williamson and Daum, *American Petroleum Industry*, 630–47.

[21]Williamson and Daum, *American Petroleum Industry*, 589–613; Nevins, *Rockefeller*, 2:3.

[22]Nevins, *Rockefeller*, 2:29–30.

[23]The Russo-American oil war was a crucial part of Rockefeller's career. My three sources for this episode, which is described in the next six paragraphs, are Ralph W. Hidy and Muriel E. Hidy, *Pioneering in Big Business, 1882–1911* (New York: Harper and Brothers, 1955), 130–54; Nevins, *Rockefeller* 1:397, 505, 666; 2:102–04, 125–26; Williamson and Daum, *American Petroleum Industry*, 509–19, 630–47.

[24]Nevins, *Rockefeller*, 2:125–26.

[25]*Ibid.*, 2:115.

[26]Hidy and Hidy, *Pioneering in Big Business*, 137.

[27]Nevins, *Rockefeller*, 1:237.

[28]*Ibid.*, 1:397, 186, 395, 627–29.

[29]*Ibid.*, 1:627–29.

[30]*Ibid.*, 1:623; 2:245–75; Hessen, *Schwab*, 24, 63–64.

[31]Nevins, *Rockefeller*, 2:295–96, 90–93; Raymond P. Fosdick, *John D. Rockefeller, Jr.: A Portrait* (New York: Harper and Row, 1956), 35.

[32]B. F. Winkelman, *John D. Rockefeller: The Authentic and Dramatic Story of the World's Greatest Money Maker and Money Giver* (Philadelphia: Universal Book and Bible House, 1937), 309.

[33]Nevins, *Rockefeller*, 1:190, 237, 627; 2:427.

[34]*Ibid.*, 2:366–68.

[35]Armentano, *Myths of Antitrust*, 75–85; John S. McGee, "Predatory Price Cutting: The Standard Oil (N. J.) Case," *Journal of Law and Economics* 1 (Oc-

tober 1958), 137–69; Hidy and Hidy, *Pioneering in Big Business*, 671–718.

[36]Nevins, *Rockefeller*, 2:479.

[37]*Ibid.*, 2:435. The Bible verses are Luke 6:38, I Timothy 6:10, and Malachi 3:10.

[38]E. Richard Brown, *Rockefeller Medicine Men: Medicine and Capitalism in America* (Berkeley: University of California Press, 1979); Alvin Moscow, *The Rockefeller Inheritance* (Garden City, N. Y.: Doubleday and Co., 1977), 101–08; Rockefeller, *Random Reminiscences*, 137–62; and Nevins, *Rockefeller*, 2:300–27, 386–402.

[39]Nevins, *Rockefeller*, 2:292–94, 199–200; Rockefeller, *Random Reminiscences*, 24–29.

[40]Fosdick, *John D. Rockefeller, Jr.*, 8–10; Nevins, *Rockefeller*, 2:199–200.

[41]John K. Winkler, *John D.: A Portrait in Oils* (New York: Blue Ribbon Books, 1929), 226. For a recent biography of Rockefeller, see Ron Chernow, *Titan* (New York: Random House, 1998). For my critical review, see "Rockefeller Biography Has Serious Flaws," *The Detroit News* (July 22, 1998), 11A.

Notes to Chapter Six

Andrew Mellon and the 1920s

[1]Andrew Mellon, *Taxation: The People's Business* (New York: Macmillan, 1924), 16.

[2]*New York Times*, December 17, 1929, p. 1. U. S. Bureau of the Census, *Historical Statistics of the United States* (Washington: Government Printing Office, 1975), 1107. See also Benjamin G. Rader, "Federal Taxation in the 1920s: A Reexamination," *The Historian* 33 (May 1971), 432; and Roy G. Blakey and Gladys C. Blakey, *The Federal Income Tax* (London: Longmans, Green and Co., 1940), 516.

Contemporary accounts of Mellon tended to treat him as either a saint or a devil. A hostile biography of Mellon is Harvey O'Connor, *Mellon's Millions: The Life and Time of Andrew Mellon* (New York: The John Day Co., 1933). For a friendly biography, see Philip H. Love, *Andrew W. Mellon: The Man and His Work* (Baltimore: F. Heath Coggins and Co., 1929). Two more recent and more scholarly studies are David E. Koskoff, *The Mellons* (New York: Thomas Y. Crowell Co., 1978); and Lawrence L. Murray III, "Andrew Mellon: Secretary of the Treasury, 1921–1932: A Study in Policy" (Ph. D. dissertation, Michigan State University, 1970).

[3]Thomas Mellon, *Thomas Mellon and His Times* (Pittsburgh: W. G. Johnston and Co., 1885), 72, 77.

[4]Ibid., 164; O'Connor, *Mellon's Millions*, 21–22, 26, 29–30, 32, 35, 49–51, 54; William Larimer Mellon, *Judge Mellon's Sons* (Pittsburgh: n. p., 1948), 28–32.

[5]Koskoff, *The Mellons*, 67–69, 172–76.

[6]Two useful books on Gulf Oil and Alcoa are Craig Thompson, *Since Spindletop; A Human Story of Gulf's First Half-Century* (Pittsburgh: n. p., 1951); Charles C. Carr, *Alcoa, An American Enterprise* (New York: Rinehart, 1952).

[7]Love, *Andrew Mellon*, 37.

[8]Mellon, *Judge Mellon's Sons*, 396–438; Koskoff, *The Mellons*, 165–67, 172–76, 182–83, 260.

[9]Bureau of the Census, *Historical Statistics*, 1104.

[10]Robert Higgs, *Crisis and Leviathan: Critical Episodes in the Growth of American Government* (New York: Oxford University Press, 1987), 97–103; Blakey and Blakey, *Federal Income Tax*, 2–20. Useful biographies of the Progressives are Harry Barnard, *Independent Man: The Life of James Couzens* (New York: Charles Scribner's Sons, 1958); Richard Lowitt, *George W. Norris: The Persistence of a Progressive, 1913–1933* (Urbana: University of Illinois Press, 1971); David Thelen, *Robert M. LaFollette and the Insurgent Spirit* (Boston: Little Brown and Co., 1976). There are also many histories of the Progressive movement and of the 1920s. See, for example, Arthur S. Link and Richard C. McCormick, *Progressivism* (Arlington Heights, Ill.: Harlan Davidson, 1983).

[11]Bureau of the Census, *Historical Statistics*, 1104, 1106, 1108, 1110; Blakey and Blakey, *Federal Income Tax*, 71–103. There are several good studies on the federal income tax. See, for example, Jerold Waltman, "Origins of the Federal Income Tax, *Mid America* 62 (October 1980), 147–60; and John F. Witte, *The Politics and Development of the Federal Income Tax* (Madison: University of Wisconsin Press, 1985).

[12]Blakey and Blakey, *Federal Income Tax*, 104–21; Higgs, *Crisis and Leviathan*, 150.

[13]Mellon, *Taxation*, 129. The continuity between Wilson's desire to cut taxes and the Republican Mellon Plan is explored in Lawrence L. Murray, "Bureaucracy and Bi-Partisanship in Taxation: The Mellon Plan Revisited," *Business History Review* 52 (Summer 1978), 200–25.

[14]Murray, "Andrew Mellon," 111–17; Mellon *Taxation*, 13.

[15]Mellon, *Taxation*, 73–83. See also Andrew W. Mellon, "The Business of Taxation," *Forum* 71 (March 1924), 346–47; Andrew W. Mellon, "High Surtaxes and Municipal Securities," *The American City Magazine* 30 (March 1924), 239–40.

[16]Mellon, *Taxation*, 199–202. The building of civic centers and football stadiums does, of course, create temporary jobs and generate some local revenue.

[17]Ibid. 78, 94, 104; Carr, *Alcoa*, 23–49, Thompson, *Since Spindletop*, 9–46. Other people also argued this idea that high taxes helped larger, established businesses perpetuate monopolies. Otto H. Kahn of the Citizen's National Committee said "high surtaxes unavoidably tend to diminish competition and to intrench [sic] and fortify those who are in established positions." *New York Times*, February 24, 1924, p. 4.

[18]Mellon, *Taxation*, 9, 16–17, 79–81, 96–97. See also Andrew W. Mellon, "Taxing Energy and Initiative," *The Independent* 112 (March 29, 1924), 168.

[19]Mellon, *Taxation*, 32; Andrew W. Mellon, "What I Am Trying to Do," *World's Work* 47 (November 1923), 73–76. The Democrats in 1924 offered the Garner Plan, which would have cut taxes on those earning under $56,000,

but would have left the tax rate on the rich at 50 percent. This approach allowed the Democrats to make the following popular appeal: "There is not a person in the country getting an income of less than $56,000 a year who is not better treated by the Democratic than by the Republican scheme." See Herbert Claiborne Pell, Jr., "Taxing the Middle Class," *Forum* 71 (March 1924), 349–53 (quotation on p. 351). See also Homer Joseph Dodge, "Which Tax Plan Do We Want?" *The Independent* 112 (March 29, 1924), 169–70.

[20]O'Connor, *Mellon's Millions*, 120.

[21]*Ibid.*, 235.

[22]Koskoff, *The Mellons*, 190–91.

[23]*Ibid.*, 191; Mellon, *Judge Mellon's Sons*, 408.

[24]Mellon, *Taxation*, 16, 69–76; Blakey and Blakey, *Federal Income Tax*, 219.

[25]Mellon, *Taxation*, 9, 54, 61–62.

[26]Belle Case LaFollette and Fola LaFollette, *Robert M. LaFollette* (New York: Macmillan, 1953), 1: 178, 480–81, 2: 743–47; Robert LaFollette, *La-Follette's Autobiography* (Madison: University of Wisconsin Press, 1968), 124; Blakey and Blakey, *Federal Income Tax*, 88, 137, 146, 180, 185, 358, 379; and *New York Times*, December 15, 1929, p. 1 and 2.

[27]Mellon, *Taxation*, 111–24.

[28]Bureau of the Census, *Historical Statistics*, 1104. Love, *Andrew Mellon*, 317; Blakey and Blakey, *Federal Income Tax*, 540.

[29]Mellon, *Taxation*, 39, 55.

[30]Koskoff, *The Mellons*, 238–40.

[31]For a helpful discussion of the tax bills in Congress, see Rader, "Federal Taxation in the 1920s," 415–35.

[32]Mellon, *Taxation*, 221. For Coolidge's support of the Mellon Plan, see *New York Times*, January 5, 1924, p. 1; January 9, 1924, p. 1; and January 12, 1924, p. 1.

[33]O'Connor, *Mellon's Millions*, 229–30; Koskoff, *The Mellons*, 230.

[34]Lillian Rogers Parks, *My Thirty Years Backstairs at the White House* (New York: Fleet Publishing Co., 1961), 184. Helpful biographies of Coolidge are Donald R. McCoy, *Calvin Coolidge: The Quiet President* (New York: Macmillan, 1967); William Allen White, *A Puritan in Babylon: The Story of Calvin Coolidge* (New York: Macmillan, 1938); and Claude M. Fuess, *Calvin Coolidge: The Man from Vermont* (Hamden, Conn.: Archon Books, 1965).

[35]Parks, *Backstairs at the White House*, 183–84; Mellon, *Judge Mellon's Sons*, 395; Irwin H. Hoover, *Forty-Two Years in the White House* (Boston: Houghton Mifflin Co., 1934), 132.

[36]Parks, *Backstairs at the White House*, 178–81; Koskoff, *The Mellons*, 183.

[37]Blakey and Blakey, *Federal Income Tax*, 251–301.

[38]Thomas B. Silver, *Coolidge and the Historians* (Durham, N. C.: Carolina Academic Press, 1982), 111; O'Connor, *Mellon's Millions*, 127; Murray, "Andrew Mellon," 127–29. Hiram Johnson weighed in with this criticism of the Mellon Plan: "The concern of this tax scheme is not for the man of small income, but for the man of large income, who can best bear the burden." *New York Times*, January 18, 1924, p. 2.

[39]Rader, "Federal Taxation in the 1920s", 433.

[40]Silver, *Coolidge and the Historians*, 112–14; Barnard, *Couzens*, 165.

[41]Silver, *Coolidge and the Historians*, 112–21. Silver's study is essential reading for historians who are trying to understand the 1920s. Mellon denied he was using refunds as a politicial weapon; he called the accusations "simply preposterous." See O'Connor, *Mellon's Millions*, 159.

[42]Mellon's audit of Progressive Senator James Couzens, of Michigan, was a political error. Couzens earned $30 million working for Henry Ford; Mellon challenged the amount of capital gains tax Couzens paid on his stock. The Board of Tax Appeals not only sided with Couzens; it said that the government owed him $900,000 for overpayment. Mellon probably felt foolish and stayed out of refund cases whenever possible. Couzens, meanwhile, won reelection to the Senate, possibly using his $900,000 refund for expenses, and kept up his attacks on Mellon. See Barnard, *Couzens*, 130, 160–67.

[43]Love, *Andrew Mellon*, 318; O'Connor, *Mellon's Millions*, 237; Koskoff, *The Mellons*, 341.

[44] From 1929 to 1935, federal revenue from personal income taxes declined from $1,095 million to $527 million, while federal revenue from excise taxes during these years increased from $539 million to $1,363 million. Of course, hard times, as well as higher taxes, contributed to the fall in revenue from personal income taxes. See Bureau of the Census, *Historical Statistics*, 1107; Koskoff, *The Mellons;* Mark Leff, *The Limits of Symbolic Reform: The New Deal and Taxation, 1933–1939* (London: Cambridge University Press, 1984); Thomas M. Renaghan, "Distributional Effects of Federal Tax Policy 1929–1939," *Explorations in Economic History* 21 (1984), 40–63; Walter K. Lambert, "New Deal Revenue Acts: The Politics of Taxation" (Ph. D. dissertation, University of Texas, 1970), 1–66.

[45]John M. Blum, William S. McFeely, Edmund Morgan, Arthur M. Schlesinger, Jr., Kenneth Stampp, C. Vann Woodward, *The National Experience*, 8th ed. (New York: Harcourt, Brace, and Jovanovich, 1993), 640.

[46]John A. Garraty, *The American Nation*, 7th ed. (New York: Harper Collins, 1991), 744.

[47]Thomas A.Baily, David M. Kennedy, and Lizabeth Cohen *The American Pageant*, 11th ed. (Boston: Houghton-Mifflin, 1998), 768.

[48]Irwin Unger, *These United States: The Questions of Our Past*, concise edition (Upper Saddle River, N.J.: Prentice-Hall, 1999), 591.

[49]The issue of changing the tax structure was widely debated during the 1996 presidential election. See, for example, "An 'Untested' Flat Tax?" *Wall Street Journal* (February 9, 1996), A12; and Daniel J. Mitchell, "Making Sense of Competing Tax Reform Plans," *The Heritage Foundation, F. Y. I.* (February 22, 1996). For a critical analysis of the income tax, see Stephen Moore, "Ax the Tax," *National Review* (April 17, 1995), 38–42.

Notes to Chapter Seven

Conclusion: Entrepreneurs vs. The Historians

[1]The term "robber barons" was in use in the early 1900s, but was popularized by Matthew Josephson, *The Robber Barons: The Great American Capitalists, 1861–1901* (New York: Harcourt, Brace, and World, 1934).

[2]John M. Blum, et al., *The National Experience,* 8th ed. (New York: Harcourt, Brace, and Jovanovich, 1993), 463.

[3]Thomas A.Bailey, David M. Kennedy, and Lizabeth Cohen *The American Pageant,* 11th ed. (Boston: Houghton-Mifflin, 1998), 540-41.

[4]Publishers are sometimes reluctant to disclose sales figures, but discussions with many publishers' representatives show clearly that these three textbooks have been among the best sellers from the 1960s through the 1990s. Bailey's former publisher, D. C. Heath, claimed that *The American Pageant* has sold over two million copies. Since the 1970s, David M. Kennedy, also of Stanford University, and Lizabeth Cohen of Harvard University have been added as co-authors.

[5]p. 471. Woodward wrote the section entitled "The Ordeal of Industrialization."

[6]John Garraty, *The American Nation,* 7th ed. (New York: Harper Collins, 1991), 519–20.

[7]The only reference to the Russo-American oil war that I found was in Robert L. Kelley, *The Shaping of the American Past,* 2nd ed. (Englewood Cliffs, N. J.: Prentice-Hall, 1978), 404.

[8]For example, Lane, *Vanderbilt;* Martin, *Hill;* Hessen, *Steel Titan.*

[9]Bailey, Kennedy, and Cohen, *The American Pageant,* 536-54. See also the tenth edition of the Bailey text, especially pp. 535-51.

[10]Bailey, Kennedy, and Cohen, *The American Pageant,* 551.

[11]For good surveys of the organizational view, see Louis Galambos, "The Emerging Organizational Synthesis in Modern American History," *Business History Review,* 44 (Autumn 1970), 279–90; and Alfred D. Chandler, Jr., "Business History as Institutional History," in George R. Taylor and

Lucius F. Ellsworth, eds. *Approaches to American Economic History* (Charlottesville, Va.: University Press of Virginia, 1971). For books that use the organizational approach, see Alfred D. Chandler, Jr., ed., *The Railroads: The Nation's First Big Business* (New York: Harcourt, Brace, and World, 1965). See also Chandler's *Strategy and Structure* (Cambridge, Mass.: MIT Press, 1962), and *The Visible Hand: The Managerial Revolution in American Business* (Cambridge, Mass.: Belknap Press, 1977). A good book on the impact of corporate organization on American society is Jerry Israel, ed., *Building the Organizational Society* (New York: Free Press, 1972), especially the essay by Samuel P. Hays, "The New Organizational Society," 1–15.

[12]Thomas, "The Automobile Industry and Its Tycoon," 141.

[13]*Ibid.*, 142.

[14]Livesay, *Carnegie*; Hessen, *Schwab*.

[15]Stephan Thernstrom, *Poverty and Progress: Social Mobility in a Nineteenth Century City* (Cambridge, Mass.: Harvard University Press, 1964); William Miller, "American Historians and the Business Elite," *Journal of Economic History* 9 (November 1949), 184–208; Edward Pessen, "The Egalitarian Myth and the American Social Reality: Wealth, Mobility and Equality in the 'Era of the Common Man'," *American Historical Review* 76 (October 1971), 989–1034. See also Frances W. Gregory and Irene D. Neu, "The American Industrial Elite in the 1870's," in William Miller, ed., *Men in Business* (Cambridge, Mass.: Harvard University Press, 1952), 193–211.

[16]Michael P. Weber, *Social Change in an Industrial Town: Patterns of Progress in Warren, Pennsylvania, from Civil War to World War I* (University Park, Pa.: Pennsylvania State University Press, 1976).

[17]Herbert Gutman, "The Reality of the Rags-to-Riches 'Myth': The Case of Paterson, New Jersey, Locomotive, Iron, and Machinery Manufacturers, 1830–1880," in Stephen Thernstrom and Richard Sennett, eds., *Nineteenth Century Cities: Essays in the New Urban History* (New Haven, Conn.: Yale University Press, 1969), 98–124; and Bernard Saracheck, "American Entrepreneurs and the Horatio Alger Myth," *Journal of Economic History* 38 (June 1978), 439–56.

[18]Ralph Andreano, "A Note on the Horatio Alger Legend: Statistical Studies of the Nineteenth Century American Business Elite," in Louis P. Cain and Paul J. Uselding, eds., *Business Enterprise and Economic Change* (Kent, Ohio: Kent State University Press, 1973), 227–46.

[19]Pessen, *Riches, Class, and Power Before the Civil War*, 303. Although I disagree with Professor Pessen's conclusions, I have learned much from reading his books and articles.

[20]Baltzell, *Philadelphia Gentlemen*; Lundberg, *The Rich and the Super-Rich*; and Ingham, *The Iron Barons*.

[21]See Lee Benson, "Philadelphia Elites and Economic Development: Quasi-Public Innovation during the First American Organizational Revolution," *Working Papers of the Eleutherian Mills-Hagley Foundation* (1978); Joseph F. Rishel, *The Founding Families of Pittsburgh: the Evolution of a Regional Elite, 1760–1810* (Pittsburgh: University of Pittsburgh Press, 1990); Frederic C. Jaher, *The Urban Establishment: Upper Strata in Boston, New York, Charleston, Chicago, and Los Angeles* (Urbana, Ill.: University of Illinois Press, 1982); and Stanley Lebergott, *Wealth and Want* (Princeton, N.J.: Princeton University Press, 1975). There are a variety of newer studies that discuss the issue of the continuity of leadership. For example, see Edward J. Davies II, "Class and Power in the Anthracite Region: The Control of Political Leadership in Wilkes-Barre, Pennsylvania, 1845–1885," *Journal of Urban History* 9 (May 1983), 291–334.

[22]See Pessen, *Riches, Class, and Power Before the Civil War*; and Pessen, The Egalitarian Myth," 1020–27; and Gabriel Kolko, *Wealth and Power in America* (New York: Frederick A. Praeger, 1962).

[23]For another essay that pursues this reasoning, see Klein, "The Robber Barons," 13–22.

[24]Holbrook, *Hill*, 201.

[25]Collier and Horowitz, *The Rockefellers*.

INDEX

Bibliographic Essay

The major sources for this book are cited in the footnotes after each chapter. In this bibliographic essay, therefore, I will briefly indicate the origins of the Robber Baron concept and then explain other useful sources in the Robber Baron controversy, some of which were written after 1987, when this book was first published.

The idea of referring to certain businessmen as robber barons is an old one. Matthew Josephson, *The Robber Barons: The Great American Capitalists, 1861-1901* (New York: Harcourt, Brace and World, 1934) popularized it for twentieth century readers, but it goes back at least 800 years before that. According to Eli Heckscher, *Mercantilism,* the Rhine River was a central trading route in Europe during the Middle Ages. During the 1100s, the Rhine had nineteen toll stations, replete with armed guards, to tax traders sending goods up and down the river. These early "robber barons" did not create wealth; they extorted it from others. They resemble America's nineteenth century robber barons—Henry Villard, Edward Collins, and Leland Stanford—who had toll stations in Washington, D.C. and assessed taxpayers to support their inefficient steamships and railroads. All of these robber barons are classic political entrepreneurs, who used politics, not innovation and low prices, to gain wealth. In the case of the medieval robber barons, the number of toll stations along the Rhine River increased to 44 in the 1200s, and to over 60 in the 1300s. Likewise in the U.S., with the growth of government in the twentieth and twenty-first centuries, the opportunities for political entrepreneurship have also increased. The key error that Josephson made was to mix both market and political entrepreneurs, and not to separate their differing impacts on American life.

The best text in U. S. business history, one that puts the Robber Baron conflict in excellent historical perspective, is Larry Schweikart, *The Entrepreneurial Adventure* (New York: Harcourt and Brace, 2000). A shorter, useful text is Gerald Gunderson, *The Wealth Creators* (New York: E. P. Dutton, 1989). A study that focuses on recent entrepreneurs, one that indirectly dispels the robber baron idea, is George Gilder, *Recapturing the Spirit of Enterprise* (San Francisco: ICS Press, 1992).

Historians often tend to be woefully trained in basic economics. Two short, helpful primers on economics are Henry Hazlitt, *Economics in One Lesson* (New York: Laissez Faire Books, [1946, 1962, 1979] 1996), a readable book that has sold one million copies; and James Gwartney and Richard Stroup, *What Everyone Should Know about Economics and Prosperity* (1993). A short and venerable primer on economics is Frederic Bastiat, *The Law,* written in 1850 and recently (1998) published by the Foundation for Economic Education, in Irvington, New York. Finally, the first two chapters of Milton and Rose Friedman, *Free to Chose* (New York: Avon Books, 1980), are an eloquent and informative introduction to economics.

The growth of government in the U. S. has spawned several important works of political philosophy. In fact, the first major contribution to political philosophy written in the United States, *The Federalist Papers* (1788), was not only a defense of the Constitution, but a response by Alexander Hamilton, James Madison, and John Jay to the question of what should be the proper role of government in American society. In the late 1800s, the increasing of subsidies to Robber Barons and other groups prompted Yale professor William Graham Sumner to defend limited government in a series of essays, recently collected and edited by Robert Bannister, entitled *On Liberty, Society, and Politics* (Indianapolis: Liberty Fund, 1992). During the rapid spurt in the growth of government during the New Deal, a devastating critique of political entrepreneurship was Walter Lippmann, *The Good Society* (Boston: Little, Brown, and Co., 1937). It was followed by Friedrich A. Hayek, *The Road to Serfdom* (Chicago: University of Chicago Press, 1944). A brief and readable defense of free markets, written by Hayek's mentor, is Ludwig Von Mises, *The Anti-Capitalistic Mentality* (South Holland, Ill.: Libertarian Press, 1972).

About the Author

BURTON W. FOLSOM, JR. is the Charles Kline professor of history and management at Hillsdale College in Michigan. He received his Ph.D. in American history from the University of Pittsburgh and has taught at the University of Nebraska, the University of Pittsburgh, Northwood University, and Murray State University. He has also been a senior fellow at the Mackinac Center for Public Policy in Midland, Michigan; and historian in residence at the Center for the American Idea in Houston, Texas.

Professor Folsom's first book was *Urban Capitalists* (Johns Hopkins University Press, 1981; second ed., University of Scranton Press, 2000). His later books include *Empire Builders* (Rhodes and Easton, 1998); *No More Free Markets or Free Beer: The Progressive Era in Nebraska, 1900-1924* (Lexington Books, 1999). He has two edited books, *The Spirit of Freedom* (Foundation for Economic Education, 1994); and *The Industrial Revolution and Free Trade* (Foundation for Economic Education, 1996). His articles have appeared in the *Journal of Southern History, Pacific Historical Review, Journal of American Studies, Great Plains Quarterly, The American Spectator,* and *The Wall Street Journal*. He is a columnist on economic history for *The Freeman* for *Ideas on Liberty.*